LAW ENFORCEMENT:
THE FEDERAL ROLE

LAW ENFORCEMENT: THE FEDERAL ROLE

Report of

The Twentieth Century Fund Task Force on the
Law Enforcement Assistance Administration

Background paper by
VICTOR NAVASKY

with DARRELL PASTER

McGraw-Hill Book Company

New York   St. Louis   San Francisco   London   Düsseldorf
Kuala Lumpur   Mexico   Montreal   Panama   São Paulo
Sydney   Toronto   New Delhi   Singapore

Library of Congress Cataloging in Publication Data

Twentieth Century Fund. Task Force on the Law
  Enforcement Assistance Administration.
  Law enforcement.

  Includes bibliographical references.
  1. United States. Law Enforcement Assistance
Administration. 2. Federal aid to law enforcement
agencies—United States. 3. Law enforcement—
United States. I. Navasky, Victor S. II. Title.
HV8143.T89 1976   353.007'4   76-12526

ISBN 0-07-065627-4
ISBN 0-07-065628-2 pbk.

Contents

For several years, the Twentieth Century Fund has supported a program of research in the area of criminal justice. Last summer, noting that the federal Law Enforcement Assistance Administration (LEAA) would be coming up for congressional authorization in 1976, the Trustees of the Fund decided that an independent examination of this agency might well contribute to public debate on its future.

Although LEAA has had its supporters as well as its critics, objective assessments of its mandate and performance are scarce. Established in 1968 as a result of intensifying public concern about the ability of state and local criminal agencies to cope with soaring crime rates, LEAA has had a troubled existence. Despite a budget that is now close to $1 billion a year, the agency has not been able to bring about a decline in crime, although some of its original sponsors—as well as some of its personnel—held out crime reduction as its major objective. Nor has the $4.5 billion that LEAA has spent served to make the criminal justice system demonstrably more humane or, at least, more efficient.

The Fund organized a Task Force made up of a diverse group of distinguished citizens, many of them with a wealth of experience in the criminal justice field, to examine LEAA. This Report represents the Task Force's consensus, achieved through long and arduous discussion, on an appropriate role for the federal government in the traditionally local activity of law enforcement.

The Task Force was enormously energetic and industrious. Despite its own substantial knowledge and wisdom, it decided to hear a series of expert witnesses including Richard Velde, the present director of the LEAA; Gerald Caplan, the head of the National Institute of Law Enforcement and Criminal Justice; Patrick Murphy, the president of the Police Foundation; and Sarah Carey, a lawyer who has written a series of reports, entitled *Law and Disorder*, dealing with the agency. The Task Force then engaged in vigorous and far-ranging debate. Views frequently clashed, but the Task Force was determined to come to an agreement on what the future should hold for LEAA. The success of the group in producing a strong and unanimous Report owes much to A. Lynwood Holton, the Task Force chairman, who seemed to have an innate sense of when constructive compromise was attainable.

The Report of the Task Force affirms both the need for and the limitations of a federal program for law enforcement. It calls for a fundamental restructuring of LEAA and its relationship with state and local agencies. Unquestionably, these recommendations are provocative, but they also are thoughtful and realistic, the product of a great deal of dedicated work.

The Fund is grateful to Governor Holton and all of the other members of the Task Force for their cooperation and hard work. They were aided in their deliberations by Victor Navasky, the author of *Kennedy Justice*, who, with Darrell Paster, wrote the background paper on LEAA that accompanies the Report of the Task Force; Mr. Navasky also served as Task Force rapporteur.

I am confident that the recommendations that follow make a strong and positive contribution toward dealing with one of the nation's most troubling and apparently intractable problems.

M. J. Rossant, **Director**
The Twentieth Century Fund
March 1976

Members of the Task Force

James Ahern
Director, Insurance Crime
Prevention Institute
Westport, Connecticut

Michael Armstrong
Attorney, Barrett, Smith,
Shapiro and Simon
New York, New York

Ilus Davis
Attorney, Dietrich, Davis,
Dicus, Rowlands
and Schmitt
Kansas City, Missouri

Martha Derthick
Senior Fellow, The Brookings
Institution
Washington, D.C.

Reverend Theodore Evans
St. Paul's Church
Stockbridge, Massachusetts

A. Linwood Holton
Chairman
Former Governor of Virginia
Attorney, Hogan and Hartson
Washington, D.C.

Hubert Locke
Former Dean of Public Affairs
and Community Service,
University of Nebraska
Omaha, Nebraska

Cecil F. Poole
Attorney, Jacobs, Sills and
Coblentz
San Francisco, California

William D. Ruckelshaus
Attorney, Ruckelshaus,
Beveridge and Fairbanks
Washington, D.C.

Robert Scott
Assistant General Counsel,
Montgomery Ward
Chicago, Illinois

LAW ENFORCEMENT: THE FEDERAL ROLE

Report of the Task Force

INTRODUCTION

During the 1960s, the crime rate in the United States began to rise dramatically. In the space of that decade, the number of robberies committed per year tripled, and the number of murders increased by 75 percent; the statistics on other crimes were equally alarming. These figures reflected, to some extent, improved techniques of crime reporting. But the actual number of crimes—especially violent crimes—committed each year increased sharply. And it is still increasing.

By the late 1960s, soaring crime rates had become a public issue, not only because of the direct harm suffered by victims but also because the police, courts, and correctional programs were overwhelmed by the numbers involved. During this period, delays in police response to crime, uneven law enforcement, overcrowded courts, and inhumane and ineffective prisons came to be acknowledged generally as public ills, and the outcry against crime in the streets became impossible for government to ignore. Both civil libertarians and advocates of "law and order" called for the federal government to assist the states and localities in their efforts to combat crime.

In 1965, in an effort to provide assistance and leadership to state and local criminal justice agencies, the federal government established the Office of Law Enforcement Assistance, which provided money, in the form of grants, to help local law enforcement. That same year, President Lyndon Johnson created the President's Commission on Law Enforcement and the Administration of Justice. In 1966, the

Commission published a report that recommended the establishment of a federal agency within the Justice Department to support local law enforcement and criminal justice efforts.

In 1968, Congress passed the Omnibus Crime and Safe Streets Act, creating the Law Enforcement Assistance Administration (LEAA) as the principal federal agency dealing with the problem of crime at the state and local levels. This agency would function, according to the provisions of the act, in five ways: (1) by supporting statewide planning in the field of criminal justice through the creation of state planning agencies; (2) by supplying the states and localities with block grants of federal funds to improve their criminal justice systems; (3) by making discretionary grants to special programs in the field of criminal justice; (4) by developing new devices, techniques, and approaches in law enforcement through the National Institute of Law Enforcement and Criminal Justice, LEAA's research arm; and (5) by supplying money for the training and education of criminal justice personnel.

The agency has now been in operation for seven years, and despite the size of its budget (it has spent $4.5 billion), the controversial nature of its programs, and continuing public concern about crime, there is no up-to-date, independent evaluation of LEAA and its effectiveness. Now Congress has before it proposed legislation to reauthorize the agency. This Task Force was established to assess LEAA's record and to make recommendations regarding its future.

THE PURPOSE OF THE AGENCY

Since LEAA's establishment, crime rates—especially for violent crime—have continued to soar (except for a brief and unexplained respite in 1972). Last year alone, reported crimes went up 18 percent, the largest increase since the Federal Bureau of Investigation (FBI) began collecting statistics almost 50 years ago. Meanwhile, all the manifest ills of the criminal justice system persist. State and local criminal justice systems remain as fragmented as ever. The courts are still overloaded; jails are still crowded; prosecutorial offices are generally underfunded; and sentencing and parole procedures and decisions remain arbitrary and uncoordinated. Nor do we know any more about the causes of crime than we did before LEAA came into being.

It would be naïve to blame LEAA for not solving these problems. Crime, after all, results from a variety of social, economic, political, psychological, and institutional forces, the relative importance of which is very hard to assess and which together resist even the most intelligent attempts at social control. It is both unrealistic and unfair to expect an agency whose budget represents only 5 percent of all state and local expenditures on law enforcement to have a significant impact on the crime statistics. But LEAA certainly is responsible for the confusion that its own rhetoric has generated regarding its purpose.

In the early 1970s, Jerris Leonard, then LEAA's administrator, proclaimed that LEAA's High Impact Cities Anti-Crime program, which involved an expenditure of $160 million in eight cities, was going to reduce crime in those cities by 5 percent in two years and 20 percent in five years. In 1972, when the national crime rate took a slight dip, LEAA did not hesitate to take the credit. In 1973, a report published by the LEAA-funded National Conference of State Criminal Justice Planning Administrators paraded charts, facts, and figures, all designed to demonstrate that "since the passage of the Safe Streets Act, the rampaging annual increase in crime has been halted and reversed."[1]

Subsequently, of course, the crime rate resumed its climb. In a recent speech, the director of the National Law Enforcement Institute observed, "Today, virtually no one—scholars, practitioners, and politicians alike—dares to advance a program which promises to reduce crime substantially in the near future."[2]

Donald Santarelli, another former LEAA administrator, has expressed the view that LEAA's purpose should be to improve the criminal justice system. It is easy to dismiss this view as a justification for institutional self-perpetuation, but it is undeniable, too, that the system has room for improvement. Police, courts, and corrections could all be both more humane and more efficient. And all could coordinate their activities more effectively than they now do. To the extent that LEAA has pursued the mirage of crime reduction, it has nurtured wishful thinking in others and has itself been diverted from the useful and critical task of discovering and promoting ways to improve and coordinate the various elements of the criminal justice system.

Implicit in all the Task Force's deliberations has been the shared assumption that, in spite of the problems that LEAA has encountered, the federal government can serve the public interest by playing a role in criminal justice and law enforcement at all levels.

Given the limitations on both the resources and the properly used powers that the federal government can bring to bear in the area, we have sought to determine what functions can be performed most effectively and constructively at the federal level, rather than at the state or local level. The recommendations that follow are based on these considerations.

At the outset, *the Task Force recommends a basic clarification of the agency's legislative mandate, eliminating the false promise of crime reduction and clearly establishing that LEAA's primary purpose is to enable the states and the local units of government to improve the effectiveness of their police, courts, and corrections agencies in dealing with crime.*

With this mandate, LEAA can begin to stimulate creative approaches at the state and local levels, where the problem of crime in the United States must ultimately be addressed. It is the hope of the Task Force that improving the criminal justice system can also have an impact on the crime rate—if not in lowering it, then in keeping it from rising more than it otherwise would. But we cannot rely on any agency or procedure specifically to reduce crime; whereas, we can rely on some measures to solve the administrative and other problems of the criminal justice system.

THE BLOCK GRANT PROGRAM

For the past two hundred years, a consensus has existed in the United States to the effect that the federal government should have a severely limited role in domestic law enforcement. The criminal justice system therefore consists, for the most part, of state and local government agencies. Accordingly, LEAA has distributed most of its money in the form of block grants so that states and localities might address their own programs in their own way.

The legislation that created LEAA required each state to establish a state planning agency (SPA) in order to participate in the program. Each year, the SPAs receive a certain amount of money ($200,000 plus an allotment based on population) to finance preparation of a plan for the use of funds in the state's criminal justice system. The plan must then be submitted to federal LEAA for approval. When the federal government certifies that the plan conforms to the criteria set forth in the legislation, it makes a block grant, based on population, to the state, which then makes its own grants to state and local agencies in its criminal justice system. The block grant system represents an attempt to reconcile the objective of enabling states and localities to control their own criminal justice programs with the objective of ensuring that federal monies are spent in accordance with certain minimal standards and program goals.

In pursuit of these objectives, LEAA has encumbered the planning process with red tape. The printed guidelines for state plans are 200 pages long. The agency has spent hundreds of thousands of man-hours and millions of dollars in bureaucratic hairsplitting with 55 state and territorial planning agencies over the adequacy of the plans. The SPAs themselves have spent hundreds of thousands of man-hours in preparing plans that, while they may or may not meet the complicated LEAA guideline requirements, frequently have little or nothing to do with the way in which the funding boards ultimately allocate the funds received from LEAA. Some state plans are the work of outside consultants who have written them to conform to LEAA guidelines rather than to the real needs and priorities of the respective states.

Viewing its primary function as passing on the block grants to the states, LEAA is reluctant to withhold funds from a state for failing to submit an adequate plan. Instead, its regional office sends the plan back to be rewritten, attaches special "conditions," or delays funding, inconveniencing all concerned. Ultimately, except in one or two cases, the federal monies have flowed forth, even for defective or inadequate plans. Thus, the federal and regional apparatus is something of a paper tiger, its negotiations with the SPAs a sort of ritualized bureaucratic dance, its threats a charade.

Moreover, instead of planning for an entire state's criminal justice budget, most SPAs plan only for the federally provided 5 percent. Instead of spending their time setting priorities and encouraging a comprehensive, coordinated approach to the problem of crime and its control at the state level, SPAs prepare paper plans and administer grants. Mayor Harvey Sloane, M.D., of Louisville, Kentucky, speaking on behalf of the National League of Cities and the United States Conference of Mayors, has testified that the red tape imposed on the current planning process has undermined the goals of that process. By the time local plans have been cleared at the substate, state, regional, and federal levels, "the whole process can take months, and more importantly, the end product often scarcely resembles the 'needs and priorities' identified by the local planning agency and local government."[3]

Improving the criminal justice system—through better trained police; speedier and fairer trials; better staffed, administered, and conceived correctional institutions and programs—is at the heart of the effort this nation needs to make in dealing with the problem of crime. The LEAA bureaucracy has contributed little to this end; in fact, a considerable body of evidence, presented during hearings held by the Task Force, indicates that LEAA's administrative maze serves, for the most part, to frustrate this objective.

The designers of LEAA's block grant system intended to stimulate statewide comprehensive criminal justice planning and to support worthwhile projects without taking criminal justice out of the hands of state and local governments and without generating the cumbersome bureaucracy that characterized most other federal grant-in-aid programs. These objectives are certainly desirable, but the block grant program has failed, for the most part, to achieve them. This failure suggests that it may be impossible to devise an administrative structure that can effectively police thousands of agencies and projects without infringing on states rights, misconstruing local priorities, invading civil liberties, or maintaining a vast, expensive, and ultimately counterproductive staff.

The Task Force, therefore, recommends that the regional bureaucracy of LEAA be dismantled and that one-half of the monies available under the law enforcement assistance program flow directly to state, county, and municipal units of government as special revenue sharing dollars to improve the criminal justice system. The money would be appropriated either to the federal agency itself or to the Treasury Department and would be distributed to the recipients according to a statutory formula. (The formula might take into account population, population density, criminal justice expenditures in the previous year, and/or crime rate.*)

The legislation that established LEAA also imposed matching requirements on the states and localities. The purpose of these requirements is to ensure that the project for which the federal funds are to be used is the object of a commitment on the part of the source of the matching funds and is not viewed merely as a way to get money from the federal government. But the requirements have served only to distort state and local priorities without furthering LEAA's purposes. *The Task Force, therefore, urges that no matching requirements be imposed on the use of these special revenue sharing funds.*

Under the Task Force proposal, states and localities would be free to spend their special revenue sharing dollars on their

---

*Some members of the Task Force, concerned that the inclusion of "crime rate" might lead jurisdictions to inflate their figures, would prefer to omit this element from the formula.

own criminal justice priorities without interference from the federal government.* Governors, mayors, and county executives would be accountable for the expenditure of those dollars, as they are for other expenditures under their jurisdiction. The actions of these chief executives may receive closer scrutiny from the public than those of state and local planning boards and agencies, which, under the current system, are largely invisible. The publicity to which chief executives are subjected and the public's ability to hold elected officials to account are probably the best safeguards available for the proper use of funds in the criminal justice system.

The sole condition attached to the special revenue sharing funds would be the recipients' agreement to give the federal agency access to their programs for the purposes of evaluation. The federal agency would publicize the findings—both positive and negative—of such evaluations for the benefit of agencies in other jurisdictions that might be contemplating similar programs.

THE STRUCTURE AND FUNCTIONS
OF FEDERAL LEAA

The Task Force recommends that the national functions of LEAA should be performed by an entity that might be called the Law Enforcement Assistance Institute (LEAI). This agency would have as its primary function research, experimentation, and evaluation at the national level. The director of LEAI should be appointed by the President and responsible to the Attorney General. The agency would directly control 50 percent of the federal appropriation for law enforcement assistance (the other 50 percent going for special revenue sharing), and the law should provide that LEAI would invest at least one-half of this amount in research, evaluation, and demonstration projects.

*The federal government would, however, be charged with enforcing Title VI of the 1964 Civil Rights Act (see p. 21). And, of course, the use of these special revenue sharing funds would be subject to audit by the General Accounting Office (GAO).

At present, most of LEAA's staff in Washington is involved in keeping track of the bureaucracy it has created. The National Institute of Law Enforcement and Criminal Justice is the one part of LEAA charged specifically with research, experimentation, evaluation, and technology transfer. Yet it accounts for less than one-twentieth of LEAA's total budget, and little attempt has been made to incorporate its findings into the criminal justice system at state and local levels.

Research and evaluation, through carefully designed demonstration projects, should be at the core of a program intended to make the criminal justice system more effective. The Task Force urges that a reorganized and restructured federal agency devote itself to a national program of criminal justice research and experimentation. *In particular, the proposed LEAI should concentrate on evaluating selected state programs in progress and should make a special effort to develop more precise techniques and strategies for this purpose.*

On the basis of the findings of its evaluation projects and other in-house research, this agency would provide basic, reliable information to state and local units of government concerning what works and what does not work in law enforcement and criminal justice. It would make technical assistance available to state, local, and regional planning agencies seeking to upgrade their own planning and evaluation capacity, and it would offer incentive grants to induce states and localities to undertake carefully designed demonstration projects with built-in data-collection features to facilitate evaluation. It would undertake to publicize and circulate throughout all the states and territories the results of its evaluations in terms of which programs were successful under what conditions. In addition, LEAI would be empowered to make incentive grants or offer technical assistance to jurisdictions that wished to set up projects patterned after those that had proven successful elsewhere. And LEAI would actively promote the use of such funds and assistance by the states and localities through field visits and a variety of outreach efforts.

In other words, the Task Force believes that LEAI should provide leadership for all the agencies of the criminal justice system. It would not *require* the states and localities to do anything other than administer their grants in accordance with the statutory provisions regarding discrimination. But through evaluation, education, example, incentives, demonstration projects, publicity, and technical assistance, LEAI would attempt to lead the way.

An example of such leadership from LEAA's own history is the independent National Advisory Commission on Criminal Justice Standards and Goals, created and funded in 1971 to develop a set of guidelines for the improvement of the criminal justice system and the reduction of crime at the state and local levels. In 1973, the commission published seven reports: *Police; Courts; Corrections; Community Crime Prevention; The Criminal Justice System; A National Strategy to Reduce Crime;* and *The Proceedings of the National Conference on Criminal Justice.* Although LEAA has disseminated the reports widely, its policy is not to endorse the specific reports or to require the states to adopt the standards and goals the commission has proposed. *The Task Force recommends that LEAI selectively endorse portions of these standards and goals reports and provide incentives for states and localities to implement them.**

COMPREHENSIVE PLANNING

Although, for practical reasons, the Task Force opposes a federal requirement that the states engage in comprehensive criminal justice planning, it endorses the idea of planning at regional, state, and local levels. Because state governors are in the best position to bring together and coordinate the various elements of the criminal justice system within their states, the Task Force especially endorses the idea of comprehensive, coordinated criminal justice planning on a statewide basis. Such planning should involve the state's entire criminal justice budget—not just the use of the proposed special revenue sharing funds.

Most experts involved in planning in the area of criminal justice believe that the present one-year planning cycle (which

---

*Some members of the Task Force believe the *Police* report, for example, to be inadequate but many of the other recommended standards and goals to be quite useful.

often, due to LEAA's changing guidelines, turns out in practice to be a six-month planning cycle) is not long enough. The Task Force agrees. So many worthwhile projects take more than a year to conceive, try out, and implement that the requirement of "annual planning" is generally counterproductive. The Task Force, therefore, endorses the idea of five-year comprehensive plans and recommends that, rather than prepare an annual comprehensive plan, those states that continue to support such planning work with the localities prepare five-year comprehensive plans and offer annual statements relating to the implementation of these plans for LEAI to consider as part of its evaluation process.

The Task Force also recommends that the proposed LEAI encourage comprehensive planning by providing funds for this purpose to those states that undertake such planning. These state plans would not be subject to prior federal approval, but from time to time during the five-year cycle of the plans, the agency would review and evaluate their implementation and provide additional funds to expand successful programs.

EARMARKED FUNDS

Although LEAA is referred to as a block grant program, Congress has required that special funds appropriated for the agency be earmarked for corrections and for juvenile justice. Under legislation currently being proposed, additional special funds would be earmarked for the courts. The Task Force believes that such earmarking is inconsistent with both the principle that states and localities should determine how their criminal justice dollars are spent and the ideal of comprehensive planning. Accordingly, *the Task Force recommends the elimination of all specially earmarked funds.*

Over the years, the police have gotten far more than their share of LEAA dollars. Congress resorted to earmarking special monies in order to redress the balance in the criminal justice system. But the validity of the end does not justify this means. Other approaches must be explored to assure that each component of the system gets fair consideration in the funding process and its fair share of funds. The Task Force believes that the federal government's role in the achievement of this goal should be the provision of education and incentives at the national level and a special revenue sharing program that locates accountability in elected officials at the state, county, and local levels.

CORRUPTION AND ORGANIZED CRIME

Precisely because it cuts across state lines and is remote from local influences, the federal government is better equipped than other levels to perform a few specific criminal justice functions. For example, organized crime is often committed on an interstate basis, and efforts to combat organized crime may be most effective if they are national in scope. The investigation of official corruption is another area in which the federal government may make a contribution. Even those state and local criminal justice officials who have nothing to hide cannot reasonably be expected to fund investigations of which they might be made targets. *The Task Force recommends that LEAI make special provision for direct federal funding of projects in these two areas.*

THE GRANTING PROCESS

The Task Force recognizes that the Justice Department and its constituent divisions and agencies are and ought to be responsive to policy initiatives from the White House. But policy initiatives are one thing; interference in the granting process is another. The Task Force has heard testimony regarding improper interference on the part of the White House in grants to a community organization in the Philadelphia area; according to this evidence, a $1 million grant, which normally might take nine months or more to negotiate and process, was put through in one day on White House orders in an attempt to secure the support of the mayor, a Democrat, for the Republican candidate in the 1972 presidential election.[4] Moreover, it is generally believed that, in both the Impact Cities and Pilot Cities programs, some demonstration sites were selected for purely political reasons, in spite of the inappropriateness of the cities for the programs, and that the programs suffered as a result of this bias in site selection.[5]

The Task Force recommends that applications for incentive awards to expand existing programs be subject to stringent and independent review procedures. Such procedures should include on-site review by LEAI research personnel as well as review by independent panels consisting of social scientists and criminal justice professionals. Proposals for research and for research-oriented demonstration projects should be subject to peer review procedures similar to those followed by the National Institute of Mental Health, whose granting process many social scientists regard as exemplary.*

IN-HOUSE RESEARCH

Although LEAA-sponsored research, particularly when university-based, has contributed to a better understanding of crime and the criminal justice system, too much reliance on outside research has made LEAA's research program diffuse and unmanageable.

The Institute of Law Enforcement and Criminal Justice,

---

*This process includes three elements: first, a number of units comprised of experts in a specific area, who have their own budget and help shape as well as administer research; second, decision-making groups referred to as "study sections," each composed of about a dozen social scientists and practitioners, who meet three or four times a year, review applications, and decide which ones should be recommended to the advisory council (in addition to the recommendation, these sections provide a detailed evaluation explaining the design of the study, the significance of the problem, and the study's relationship to various problem areas; they also make site visits where necessary and assign a priority to each proposal); and third, an advisory council made up of citizens, policymakers, and senior researchers, which undertakes final review of research projects and has virtual veto power over those that do not measure up.

LEAA's research arm, has not functioned in coordination with the rest of the LEAA program. Little institute-sponsored research has found its way down to the states, far less to the streets. In seven years, although it has sponsored some valuable ad hoc research, the institute has found out little about the causes of crime that were not known when LEAA was founded. This failure may be traced to a number of causes: the state of the art of research in the social sciences; the complexity of the problem; the already-mentioned confusion of goals; the lack of an overall research strategy; and, perhaps, the personal tensions between various directors and administrators. It must also be noted that the institute has been reluctant to build up a staff of in-house researchers, on the theory that first-rate talent will not want to work for the government. *But it is the opinion of the Task Force that the proposed LEAI can attract the high-quality personnel it needs to carry out its mandate only by establishing its own research program with its own research agenda. In addition to providing grants to outside experts for research and evaluation purposes, LEAI should expand and upgrade its own research staff so that it can evaluate state and local programs and conduct research on crime, its causes, and its prevention.*

THE LAW ENFORCEMENT EDUCATION PROGRAM

At present, LEAA spends over $40 million per year paying for the education of approximately 100,000 individuals "employed in or preparing for employment in criminal justice agencies." The agency's Law Enforcement Education Program (LEEP) conducts this education effort through payments to institutions rather than to individuals. The statute requires participating institutions to establish or maintain programs leading to a degree or a certificate in areas directly related to law enforcement and criminal justice. Given this opportunity to obtain funds at a time of fiscal crisis, many educational institutions have hurriedly established a series of jerry-built programs "related" to law enforcement and criminal justice. Although LEAA has formulated criteria involving such matters as the size and location of the institution and although LEEP funds have led to the creation of some good programs, the agency has certified and financed the LEEP programs without auditing them for quality. According to a report by the GAO, on one occasion nine people processed 900 institutional applications in three days.[6]

The average policeman who participates in one of these special educational programs frequently finds himself segregated from the non-law enforcement students at the institution in which he is enrolled. At best, participants in LEEP programs get law enforcement training, but they do not really get the benefits of either a college education or a learning experience in a context that might broaden their intellectual perspectives and alert them to concerns not generally associated with the law enforcement community. The Task Force believes that special education in criminal justice is best left to the regular training programs of criminal justice agencies and that the purpose of sending people to college should be to provide them with the education that they desire. *The Task Force, therefore, recommends that LEEP's provisions be revised so that payments are made directly to individuals instead of to institutions, enabling those individuals to attend the college and pursue the curriculum of their choice. Such a program should be available to all individuals who make a commitment to a career in criminal justice.**

The Task Force makes this recommendation not because it considers criminal justice personnel entitled to a special break but because the education available at a liberal arts institution can enhance the sensitivity and competence of personnel in the criminal justice system and, hence, improve their work.

President Ford has recently proposed elimination of LEEP's budget allocation. This proposal is a response to valid criticisms of the program. But despite its failings, the program has been one of LEAA's most constructive and successful efforts. Many of its former participants feel strongly that the

---

*Apart from limiting participation in the program to individuals already employed in the criminal justice system, the Task Force has not dealt with the criteria that should be applied to potential recipients of LEEP funds.

education they received has improved their job performance.[7] The proposal to eliminate LEEP threatens to curtail the educational opportunities of police officers and other criminal justice personnel at precisely the time when the complexities of their jobs demand the breadth of exposure available only through continuing education. Therefore, *the Task Force opposes the abolition of LEEP.*

CRIMINAL JUSTICE STATISTICS

One of the positive results of the LEAA-SPA funding process is the development of a community of criminal justice planners and researchers. A recurrent theme in the literature of this community is the inadequacy of existing criminal justice statistics. For years, the FBI has compiled annual Uniform Crime Reports, but the utility of these figures as an index of real crime is in doubt. The Uniform Crime Reports are based on local police reports, which vary in quality and integrity. Recently, LEAA has sponsored victimization surveys, which have provided yet another perspective on the dimensions of crime in the United States but do not come close to satisfying the need for a systematic, regularized, reliable set of criminal justice statistics. As a general proposition, the Task Force believes that it is unwise to place the responsibility for collecting and auditing statistics in agencies whose performance and/or funding may be affected by them. *The Task Force, therefore, recommends that the agency analyze the quality, methodology, categories, and validity of existing crime statistics and give high priority and devote increased resources to the development of a more reliable and regular set of criminal justice statistics.*

INFORMATION SYSTEMS AND THE AGENCY

In 1969, LEAA organized Project SEARCH (System for Electronic Analysis and Retrieval of Criminal Histories), which underwrote and standardized the adoption of computer technology and information systems by the states and localities. At the time, only 10 states had such systems. By 1973, LEAA had spent over $50 million for this purpose, and in 1974, over 400 different systems were in use in all 50 states and at all levels of government, slightly over half of them operating at the local level. These systems have enabled police in Iowa to find out quickly and easily whether or not a person in custody has a criminal record in Georgia. They are helping to solve many other administrative problems of the criminal justice system.

The idea of using computers to streamline some of the operations of the criminal justice system was both sound and useful, and LEAA deserves credit for the resulting improvements in record keeping and enhanced access to information. But the systems now have a vast potential (which has never been systematically explored) for abuse and privacy invasion on a nationwide scale. One watchdog group has commented:

> Computer systems are characterized by central storage, efficient linkage to other agencies and data bases, and rapid and widespread access. The tendency toward central storage magnifies the consequences of damage to, or destruction of, storage facilities, and the improved efficiency of the system greatly increases the danger that inaccurate data will be widely disseminated, or that data will become available for a purpose other than that for which it was appropriately collected. Thus, although security and privacy problems existed and still exist in manual systems, there is no question that the growing use of computers and other automated processing equipment produces a fundamental change in both the likelihood and consequences of these problems.[8]

Although Project SEARCH included a program that drafted guidelines for the protection of privacy in the collection and dissemination of arrest and conviction records, LEAA has not required state and local agencies to adopt these procedures as a prerequisite for getting LEAA funding for communications systems, nor has it indicated any other steps that it might take to enforce compliance.

Because LEAA was instrumental in creating this potentially dangerous national information network, it has a special obligation to take action to see that the information is not abused. *The Task Force urges the agency to promulgate and enforce the strictest possible privacy and security safeguards and to prevent the misuse of these data by potential employers, schools, creditors, credit agencies, and insurers. The Task Force further recommends that LEAI play a leading role in educating the public as to the issues involved in this highly complex and volatile field.*

But LEAA is not the only agency in the field. The FBI has been setting up a computer system. The two agencies are now vying for control of the nationwide computerized criminal histories network. The Task Force takes no position on which agency of government should be responsible for this network. But it is obvious that these data are highly vulnerable to exploitation and abuse. Accordingly, *the Task Force recommends that a review board be established to monitor the uses, practices, and policies of the operation. It is critical that the review board be truly independent of the operating agency so that it will have the distance and freedom it needs to perform its oversight function without constraint.*

THE AGENCY AND DISCRIMINATION

At present, members of minority groups are overrepresented in the criminal justice statistics as both victims and perpetrators, relative to their share of the general population, and underrepresented among personnel at all levels of the criminal justice system. But although LEAA has one of the strongest antidiscrimination mandates of any agency in the federal government, it has been slow to act in this area. At present, for instance, the agency requires grant recipients to file an equal employment opportunity plan but makes no effort to see that such plans actually are put in operation.

The agency has yet to terminate grants on its own initiative to any of the agencies it funds for reasons of discrimination. When asked why LEAA does not pursue its antidiscrimination mandate more vigorously, LEAA officials say that their primary job is to get the money out to the states, not to withhold it, that the Civil Rights Compliance Office is understaffed, or that LEAA cannot be expected to alter local practices when its grants are so small a fraction of local spending.

The Task Force believes that funding policies that support discriminatory enforcement agencies and practices are incompatible with the goal of improving the criminal justice system. *The Task Force recommends that LEAA (1) set an example by hiring more minority group members and women; (2) supply technical assistance to those agencies claiming an inability to recruit among these groups in adequate numbers; (3) enforce Title VI of the 1964 Civil Rights Act with regard to those state and local agencies that maintain patterns and practices of discrimination, invoking, where appropriate, its ultimate weapon, grant termination; and (4) encourage states and localities to develop programs located in and dealing with the problems of high-crime, inner-city areas, taking advantage of minority expertise and personnel and providing information about the causes, costs, and prevention of crime.*

REAUTHORIZATION OF THE AGENCY

Congress has never conducted a thorough investigation of LEAA. And no reliable inventory now describes with accuracy the nature, far less the degree of success or failure, of the 105,000 grants LEAA has funded to date. In response to earlier criticisms, LEAA set up a Grants Management Information System (GMIS), which is now the primary source of information about what LEAA has funded. But the GMIS figures are of questionable utility; grant descriptions on the GMIS are written by the grantees and not checked for accuracy; the categories into which projects are divided are imprecise and overlapping; and the same grant is frequently (but not invariably) listed in more than one category. Moreover, the system's coding procedures are informal, subjective, and unreliable. The agency does not require states to supply data for the system. And the National Center for State Courts has demonstrated that the GMIS information is incompatible and inaccurate. As of February 14, 1975, LEAA could account for only 39.9 percent of its fiscal 1974 Part C (action, as opposed to planning) block grant funds and for only 75 percent of its 1973 Part C block grant funds, although 90.2 percent of the money had been spent.

Because of its failure to monitor or investigate the agency and its activities thoroughly, Congress must bear its share of the responsibility for LEAA's problems. As yet, no independent congressional fact-finding has established the degree to which LEAA's policy goals have been flouted, compromised, or realized. Yet, independent of Congress, there is substantial evidence that LEAA, as currently structured and administered, has generally failed to carry out the mission Congress gave it. On the basis of this evidence, and whether or not its other recommendations are accepted, *the Task Force urges that Congress exercise more vigorous oversight regarding LEAA.*

The administration has proposed that LEAA be authorized in 1976 for five years at a budget of $1.3 billion per year. *The Task Force opposes five-year authorization at this time without a thorough restructuring of LEAA to eliminate its serious problems and weaknesses.* The Task Force has designed its recommendations to bring about such restructuring.

If LEAA and its program are restructured, Congress should carefully monitor the operations of the federal agency and review the findings of its evaluations of state and local programs. *If the agency is not restructured, then this Task Force urges only a one- or two-year authorization, a cutback in the proposed level of authorization, and a thorough congressional investigation of LEAA.*

CONCLUSION

In the seven years it has been in operation, LEAA has been the object of considerable criticism. Although some of this criticism is politically inspired or simply unfounded, LEAA's performance has left much to be desired. Nonetheless, the Task

Force believes that the federal government can plan a positive role in nationwide law enforcement.

Ensuring that each of the numerous state, county, and local agencies responsible for criminal justice spends the federal funds it receives wisely and well is probably impossible, but the Task Force believes that the criminal justice system urgently needs money, assistance, and information and that the states and localities should not be hindered in setting their priorities.

The Task Force would prefer, of course, that federal funds be used for constructive programs rather than, as too often in the past, for showy but unnecessary hardware. The Task Force also would prefer the states and localities to make a serious commitment to comprehensive planning. But since the federal government cannot effectively enforce compliance with these objectives, it should do what it can—supply the funds and the intellectual leadership that are necessary to improve the criminal justice system and may be sufficient for that purpose if the states and localities have the will to use them effectively. Without this will, even the most interventionist federal program cannot succeed.

Until relatively recently, it was fashionable in some circles to treat law enforcement as a dirty business involving the persecution by uniformed "hard hats" of those poorer and weaker than themselves. Today, the realization has dawned that crime has victims and that the function of law enforcement and criminal justice is as much to protect the innocent as to punish the guilty. Consideration of the broader issues of this function is difficult for those who are caught up in its daily routine and struggling to handle the problems they face in the most expedient and familiar way. The federal government has a role to play precisely because it is distant from this daily routine and can make available without coercion—to the typical overworked, understaffed police chief, for example—fresh perspectives and the financial means to apply them. The Task Force has devoted its efforts to outlining a federal program that would serve both the law enforcement community and the American people as a force for both humaneness and efficiency.

NOTES

[1] National Conference of State Criminal Justice Planning Administrators, *State of the States on Crime and Justice: An Analysis of State Administration of the Safe Streets Act* (Frankfort, Ky.: National Conference of State Criminal Justice Planning Administrators, June 1, 1973), p. ii.

[2] Gerald M. Caplan, "'Losing' the War on Crime," Address at the Town Hall of California, Los Angeles, Calif., Dec. 9, 1975, p. 2.

[3] Testimony of Mayor Harvey Sloane, M. D., on behalf of the National League of Cities–U.S. Conference of Mayors, before the Subcommittee on Criminal Laws and Procedures of the Senate Judiciary Committee, Oct. 9, 1975.

[4] Testimony of Egil Krogh in hearings held by the Twentieth Century Fund Task Force on the Law Enforcement Assistance Administration, New York, N. Y., Jan. 9, 1976.

[5] General Accounting Office, *The Pilot Cities Program: Phaseout Needed Due to Limited National Benefits*, B-171019, Feb. 3, 1975.

[6] General Accounting Office. *Problems in Administering Programs to Improve Law Enforcement Education*, GGD-75-67, June 11, 1975.

[7] Ibid.

[8] SEARCH Group, Inc., *Standards for Security and Privacy of Criminal Justice Information*, Technical Report No. 13, Sacramento, Calif., Oct. 1975, p. 1.

Background Paper

*By Victor S. Navasky
with Darrell Paster*

ACKNOWLEDGMENTS

Although no definitive studies of the Law Enforcement Assistance Administration are available, a number of experts on different aspects of this complex agency have emerged. Those whose comments were particularly helpful to me include Carl Stenberg, Sarah Carey, Mae Churchill, Robert Cushman, Susan White, Gordon Zenk, Robert Crew, Charles D. Weller, Richard P. Nathan, and Richard E. Larson. Needless to say, none of them is responsible for either the conclusions or the formulations of my paper.

The members of the Task Force, especially Martha Derthick and Hubert Locke, provided many valuable comments on the paper. Reed Dewey assisted in gathering and analyzing materials, and special notice is due my secretary, Madge Spitaleri, who, with efficiency and cheerfulness, helped me prepare the manuscript. I wish to thank the Russel Sage Foundation, where I am serving as a Visiting Scholar, for the use of its facilities throughout the preparation of this paper. I wish to thank the Law Enforcement Assistance Administration itself for its full cooperation. And finally, I am indebted to my colleague, Darrell Paster, who researched this paper, prepared first drafts of a number of subsections and is primarily responsible for the material on computerized crime information systems. Joan Paster should also be thanked for emergency typing and miscellaneous assistance.

Victor S. Navasky
March 1976

Seven years ago, Congress passed the controversial Omnibus Crime Control and Safe Streets Act of 1968, which created the Law Enforcement Assistance Administration (LEAA) as part of the U.S. Department of Justice.[1]

Between its initial authorization and fiscal 1975, LEAA's budget grew from $60 million to $886 million. This year, Congress will decide whether or not to refund the agency for another five years at a proposed cost of $6.8 billion.[2]

With its appropriations, LEAA has supplied the state of Louisiana with an armored personnel carrier called "Big Bertha" and funded such programs as SWAT (Special Weapons and Tactics) in Los Angeles, STRESS (Stop the Robberies, Ensure Safe Streets) in Detroit, SCAT (Special Crime Attack Team), and ESCORT (Eliminate Street Crimes on Residential Thoroughfares) in Denver.[3] It has given $209,100 to the Association of Junior Leagues "to serve as catalysts in mobilizing community participation in organizing efforts to seek criminal justice improvements" and $239,700 to Loyola University in Los Angeles "to assess the need" for a loose-leaf encyclopedia on law enforcement. It sent three Los Angeles police captains to the Virgin Islands for one year to "upgrade administrative and operational capabilities of the police division of the department of public safety." The agency has provided walkie-talkies and communications and information equipment and more comfortable shoes for policemen across the nation, a riot-control program for the state of Maine, a Dale Carnegie course for policemen from Kentucky, and

$157,316 to the district attorney of New York County for electronic surveillance equipment, as well as "buy" and "front" money "to facilitate purchase of contraband and to otherwise assist law enforcement officers." It has helped develop a wristwatch that sends beeps—although only within a radius of 500 feet—when its wearer is in trouble. The agency also has developed a Prosecutor Management Information System (PROMIS), a computerized system designed to alleviate scheduling difficulties for prosecutors by supplying them with complete defendant background information, crime-specific data, and a summary of prior court events; it has funded a public-defender service in the District of Columbia and a volunteer probation-counselor program in Lincoln, Nebraska, which pairs high-risk youthful offenders on probation with lay persons from the community who have been trained in counseling skills. Also, it has supported such worthwhile undertakings as antifraud divisions, juvenile diversion programs, and community-based corrections facilities. At this writing, the enterprises it has funded number 105,000.

Since its inception, LEAA has been the subject of considerable controversy. Its critics charge that it is a bureaucratic nightmare and/or the forerunner of a national police force, while its supporters claim that it is the best hope for improving law enforcement and reducing crime in the United States.

The original legislation was based on the assumptions that crime control is and ought to be a state and local matter and that statewide planning is the key to improving the criminal justice system. But over the years, Congress has earmarked certain funds for certain purposes. At present, LEAA spends about one-third of its annual appropriation on direct grants and on its own programs; it passes the remaining two-thirds on to the planning agencies of the states, which then determine how those so-called block grants are to be spent.

THE ORGANIZATIONAL STRUCTURE

Federal LEAA, which is primarily a grant-making agency, employs 822 people, has $810,677,000 to spend in 1976, and consists of five main operating parts: the block grant program (current budget $452.4 million); the discretionary fund grants ($118.5 million); the National Institute of Law Enforcement and Criminal Justice ($32 million); education and training programs ($43 million); and the Juvenile Justice Office, which was created by statute in 1974 and began operation only in late 1975.

The Block Grant Program   The theory of the block grant program is that states are in the best position to encourage or require the coordination or pooling of activities among the three main components of the criminal justice system—police, courts, and corrections. Federal LEAA, therefore, distributes 85 percent of its program or "action" funds to state planning agencies (SPAs).

Each state has had to establish an SPA and has done so in order to participate in the program. Each SPA is automatically entitled to at least $200,000, plus an allotment based on population, for planning purposes; the SPA must pass along part of its planning allotment to units of general or local government for their planning.

The legislation has also attached matching requirements to the federal funds. States are required to provide one-tenth of the planning money and one-quarter of the nonfederal funding of local projects.

Federal LEAA is divided into 10 national regions. Each year, the individual SPA must submit a plan to its regional office to be certified as "comprehensive" according to the criteria set forth in the legislation.[4] When the regional office approves the plan, LEAA makes a block grant to the SPA according to a formula based on a state's population. Thus in 1974, California got $46.5 million; Massachusetts, $13.3 million. When the SPA receives the block grant, it in turn makes grants directly to state and local police, courts, corrections, or other criminal justice programs or agencies.[5] In addition, some of the less populous states receive supplements from the LEAA discretionary fund for their block grants.

The legislation that created LEAA stipulates that 50 percent of the members of the state boards, which oversee the regional plans, must be locally elected officials. The purpose of this provision is to involve officials from fields other than law enforcement in the process of determining the disposition of LEAA funds. But LEAA's counsel has interpreted the language of the statute to include sheriffs, judges, and district attorneys. Critics point out that as a result, law enforcement officials are overrepresented on regional and state planning agencies. A recent survey of the National Association of Regional Councils suggests, in fact, that only three states have provided adequate non-law enforcement representation on the councils.[6]

Discretionary Grants The federal government is supposed to use the remaining 15 percent of all action funds for grants to encourage innovative projects, to establish national priorities, to correct imbalances in state programs, or simply to fund projects that fall outside a given state's planning priorities. But discretionary grants often conflict with and sometimes confuse the SPA-granting process. Although much of this money is disbursed through LEAA's regional offices, a locality may use discretionary grants to "end run" its own state agency.

The National Institute of Law Enforcement and Criminal Justice The National Institute of Law Enforcement and Criminal Justice was originally conceived as a prestigious research institution like the National Institute of Mental Health. Its objective was "to encourage research and development and to improve and strengthen law enforcement"[7] through the granting of funds for research, the undertaking of its own research and studies, and the examination of "behavioral research on the causes and prevention of crime."[8] The institute was to make policy recommendations, establish special workshops to disseminate its findings, and carry out regional training programs for state and local criminal justice personnel. Its performance, however, is more modest.

Although its current budget is $32 million and although it does support nine rotating Visiting Fellows per year, the institute does none of its own research. For the most part, it makes research grants. But the findings of this research have had little effect on the distribution of LEAA's discretionary grants and virtually no impact on the states' use of block grants. The institute has funded such ambitious projects as the Career Criminal program (with grants totaling $2.3 million going to help prosecutors in six cities identify and quickly prosecute violent habitual criminals) and the Defensible Space project (which shows, among other things, that architectural design is a critical element in the security of apartment dwellers). But much of the institute's resources have gone into the development of equipment such as the bulletproof clothing worn by the President, a wristwatch to measure a law officer's pulse rate, and the means to assess the speed at which steel-belted radial tires can safely be used on the highways. In response to congressional criticism, the institute has begun a number of evaluation programs. It also runs the Office of Technology Transfer, whose purpose it is to encourage the replication of worthwhile programs. It conducts training programs and administers the National Criminal Justice Reference Service, which is, in effect, LEAA's bookstore and lending library.

Education and Training The agency's education and training program has four parts: the Law Enforcement Education Program (LEEP), the National Criminal Justice Educational Consortium, the Graduate Research Fellowship program, and the Internship program. The primary purpose of LEEP is to give criminal justice personnel a college education, but the great bulk of the monies has been used for police training within a college environment. In 1974, its peak year, LEEP distributed $44 million in the form of student loans and scholarships (paid directly to certified institutions) and supported some 95,000 students in colleges and universities.

The National Criminal Justice Educational Consortium was established with funds that LEAA provided to seven universities to develop and strengthen the criminal justice curricula. The seven are Arizona State, Eastern Kentucky, Michigan State, Northeastern, Portland State, the University of Maryland, and the University of Nebraska at Omaha.

The Graduate Research Fellowship program is a low-budget affair, providing grants to universities for doctoral candidates in the criminal justice area who have completed all of their graduate work except for their dissertations. The Internship program, equally small, provides weekly $65 supplements to students (undergraduate, graduate, and professional) for eight weeks while they work in various criminal justice agencies. In 1974, approximately 770 interns participated in the program.

THE PROBLEM

Critics have pointed out that during LEAA's seven years of operation, crime rates have escalated, conditions in jails and prisons have not been noticeably improved, and abuse of justice continues in docket-jammed courts. To be sure, states may now have increased capability to engage in planning in the area of criminal justice, but by and large, they have not demonstrated that the planning does much good. The Lawyers' Committee for Civil Rights Under Law has argued that "LEAA has not yet exercised the leadership mandated by Title I's design."[9] A subcommittee of the House Government Operations Committee has documented numerous instances of inefficient, wasteful, or corrupt use of block grant funds.[10] The Office of Management and Budget has concluded that

> LEAA funds have been used for projects which have little or no relationship to improving criminal justice programming. Funds are so widely dispersed that their potential impact is reduced, and the absence of program evaluation severely limits the agency's ability to identify useful projects and provide for their transfer, and too frequently LEAA funds have been used to subsidize the procurement of interesting but unnecessary equipment.[11]

Spokesmen for the cities charge that they are too remote from the planning process to affect it and that too little of the money reaches urban areas, where most crime, especially violent crime, takes place. In addition to complaining that the courts are underfunded, Chief Justice Hefflin of Alabama, representing the Association of State Chief Justices, notes that the way in which LEAA is organized forces state court systems and judges to engage in political competition for federal funds and thus "affords the opportunity for the exertion of political pressures on judges."[12] Local officials have suggested that the "match" provisions of the act (requiring localities to put up 25 percent hard cash before they can get money) make many experimental projects impossible. Today, as LEAA's critics see it, the criminal justice system is still fragmented.

To these charges LEAA supporters respond by pointing out that too much may have been expected of LEAA. Funds from LEAA make up only 5 percent of the average state's criminal justice budget and represent little more than 10 percent of the amount that the federal government disburses in its General Revenue Sharing program. (In 1973, for instance, LEAA disbursed approximately $680 million, as compared with the $6.6 billion disbursed in general revenue sharing.) The agency attributes its shortcomings to inexperience, noting that, where weaknesses have been pointed out (as in LEAA's auditing and evaluation procedures and in the need for more money in high-crime areas), the agency has moved vigorously to improve its performance. Typically, after the courts began lobbying for a provision in the statute granting them a fixed percentage of action funds as their "fair share," LEAA allocated an extra $2 million to support state court planning.[13]

Supporters of LEAA also point to its intangible impact. For example, because of LEAA, the various components of the criminal justice community are now talking to each other. Agency supporters argue that what may appear to be failings of the federal agency are actually, in many cases, by-products of the block grant system, in which decisions must be made at the state and local levels. In addition, they point out that many LEAA programs and experiments, especially in the development of community-based corrections programs (designed to rehabilitate and treat offenders near their homes), crime prevention, and so-called target hardening (physical crime prevention techniques, such as locks and lights), have been so effective that they are being adopted on a nationwide basis. And although they deplore the lack of coordination, they cite the continued fragmentation of the criminal justice system as evidence that fears of a national police network or of the undermining of separation of powers are unwarranted. As Richard Harris, chairman of the National Conference of State Planners, puts it:

> The federal money represents almost the only funds available to line-up criminal justice agencies for experimentation and attempting new ideas and techniques. . . . At this particular time in our recessionary economy, reductions in or termination of funds to states and localities would have a ripple effect. The states and localities have in many cases already cut their operations and programming to the bare bones.[14]

Congress has before it legislation that would extend LEAA's life for another five years and authorize funding of over $1 billion a year (a budget more than twice the size of the Federal Bureau of Investigation's (FBI) and representing half the total funding of the entire Justice Department). But until now, Congress has not yet held the sort of searching, systematic hearings that might provide the basis for an informed judgment regarding how and on what LEAA has spent its money over these past seven years. The program gets no closer scrutiny at the state level, since most state officials are happy simply to have the money. With the general retrenchment in foundation funding, another potential monitor of the LEAA program, the academic community, is left in the conflict-of-interest position of being forced to apply for support from the agency it might otherwise criticize. As a result, or perhaps coincidentally, the major academic evaluations of LEAA have been funded by the agency itself. The agency, incidentally, is quite open about its operation, but the data that it exuberantly shares with potential critics are of dubious value. LEAA is, for instance, quite willing to turn over a computer printout listing its 105,000 grants, but the information on the printout consists exclusively of project titles and descriptions provided by grantees. The National Center for State Courts has shown that LEAA's own statistics and data-retrieval systems are too sloppy, overlapping, and incomplete to provide the basis for serious analysis, but no better information is available.

Finally, although a number of evaluations of different parts of the LEAA program are in the works and may provide some useful background, insights, and data, they cannot really be expected to provide any definitive critique of the program. LEAA has funded at least 32 projects designed to improve and implement the evaluation of its programs. These projects include the Advisory Commission on Intergovernmental Relations' evaluation of the planning and program process, the National Academy of Science's study of the National Institute, the MITRE Corporation's evaluation of the Impact program, and the American Institute of Research's evaluation of the Pilot Cities program. Executive Management Services, Inc., is preparing an evaluation of the evaluators that attempts to integrate their findings (originally due to be finished February 28, 1976). But critics have found in the LEAA evaluations, as elsewhere in the social sciences, (1) imperfections in the state of the art of evaluation, which permit evaluations to be used to justify projects rather than judge them; (2) inaccuracies and inadequacies in obtaining and keeping crime statistics; (3) unqualified evaluators; (4) data bases (provided by LEAA or the SPAs) that are suspect either because of inefficient record keeping or for bureaucratic, political, or other self-interest reasons; (5) a dearth of "process evaluation," which would tell *why*, rather than merely *whether*, a program has or has not worked.

Relative to other agencies its size, LEAA, which receives half of the Justice Department's budget, has been underscrutinized. In LEAA's early years, two public-interest organizations took serious looks into the agency: one, the Committee for Economic Development, recommended its abolition and proposed an alternative independent agency; and the other, the Lawyers' Committee for Civil Rights Under Law, issued a series of critical reports emphasizing, but not restricted to, the civil rights aspects of the operation.[15] In 1971, Congressman John S. Monagan (D. Conn.) held hearings that exposed some of LEAA's inefficiencies and absurdities, but these hearings did not really constitute a systematic assessment of the agency.[16]

In 1973, Congressman Peter W. Rodino, Jr. (D. N.J.) held hearings that provided a forum for some of LEAA's critics but were not an attempt at a systematic critique.[17] Although the Senate Subcommittee on Criminal Laws and Procedures has been holding some pro forma hearings, they have done no more than skate over the surface of the agency.[18] The Office of Management and Budget (OMB) and the Justice Department have each completed reports on the agency—although the Attorney General has rejected the recommendations for structural changes made in the Justice Department report—neither of which is available to the general public.[19] The General Accounting Office (GAO) has issued a series of technical reports critical of various LEAA programs.[20] What press coverage there is has concentrated on gadgetry and personality conflicts within the agency.

But the available evidence does suggest some hypotheses: (1) that LEAA's mandate is so ambiguous and possibly contradictory that it has led to confusion in the operation and public understanding of the program and to such misallocation of resources as the disproportionate share of funds that has gone to the police (between 60 and 80 percent in the early years of the program); (2) that bureaucratic and political imperatives, as well as personal considerations, have worked to undermine what otherwise might have been constructive aspects of LEAA's program; and (3) that the block grant program, caught halfway between the Great Society and the New Federalism, may have been flawed in its conception because the amount of federal administrative regulation required may prove disproportionate to the benefits the program confers. There is no definitive analysis comparing LEAA's efficiency with that of other federal programs, but no one (including members of LEAA's staff) has claimed that there is not room for significant improvement at LEAA.

The Law Enforcement Assistance Administration has undoubtedly made possible hundreds of worthy projects. They include practical prescriptions on how to discourage burglars (by engraving your valuables); such important if still imperfect research as the criminal victimization studies, which try to discover the real amount of unreported crime through random surveys of citizens and businesses; the recently published nine-city study by Professor Sheldon Krantz of the Boston University Law School Center for Criminal Justice, which documents the way in which—despite the 1972 Supreme Court decision guaranteeing indigents the right to counsel— the poor have been left out in the legal cold[21]; and a series of grants totaling $6.6 million awarded to five states and one county to remove status offenders (truants, runaways, and incorrigibles) from detention and correction facilities and provide them with alternative noninstitutional treatment. Now, however, LEAA's supporters have the burden of demonstrating that the preponderance of its $4.5 billion has been wisely spent or, at least, that it has been invested with sufficient prudence and sensitivity to justify the additional investment of $6.8 billion that the Ford administration bill proposes. The agency has yet to prove its case.

II / *The Mandate*

From the first, LEAA has suffered from ambiguity of purpose. Confusion about the agency's mandate has almost certainly affected its performance and is discernible both in the agency's legislative history and in the history of the federal government's involvement with crime and law enforcement legislation.

Traditionally, crime control has been treated as a state and local problem, with no natural role for the federal government beyond the enforcement of federal statutes. In the early 1960s, Attorney General Robert F. Kennedy mounted a national campaign against organized crime, but he was always careful to stress the *organized*.[1] He also appointed Francis A. Allen, Sunderland Professor of Law of the University of Michigan, to head a committee to study the problems of the poor in obtaining justice in the federal courts. The work of the Allen committee resulted in the establishment of an Office of Criminal Justice and some reforms in bail and sentencing procedures as well. But Kennedy never portrayed street crime as a national issue.

In his 1964 presidential campaign, Barry Goldwater talked of "the growing violence in our streets" and made "law and order" a public issue. President Johnson effectively rebutted Goldwater by asserting that his administration's antipoverty and other Great Society programs were, in effect, crime-reduction efforts. But in May 1965, he delivered a Special Message to Congress on Law Enforcement and Administration of Justice, which introduced legislation that created the Office *39* of Law Enforcement Assistance (OLEA), a precursor of LEAA. The OLEA program emphasized experimentation, training, innovation, and the dissemination of knowledge.[2] The OLEA staff saw its role as "limited to the stimulation of new knowledge . . . and experimentation designed to 'show the way' rather than 'shoulder the load.'"[3] Funded at a level of about $7 million a year, OLEA carried on no program of its own but made direct grants to state, local, and private agencies and institutions. Fifty-one percent of the recipients were state, local, or county units of government, and over 25 percent were institutions of higher learning.[4]

In July 1965, Lyndon Johnson created the President's Commission on Law Enforcement and the Administration of Justice under Nicholas deB. Katzenbach. A year later, the Commission issued its report, which recommended, among other things, expanded federal support for local law enforcement and the establishment of LEAA. In support for this recommendation, the Commission argued: (1) that crime is a highly mobile, national problem and that the failure of criminal justice institutions in one state endangers citizens in other states; (2) that, in terms of simple economy, some needs are best met on the national level; and (3) that most local communities are hard pressed to afford the present costs of justice and cannot finance experimental and innovative programs. The Commission also recommended that the proposed federal crime program be administered by a presidential appointee (with the attendant prestige) working in the Justice Department under the Attorney General.

The perspective of the President's Crime Commission is suggested by its first recommendation—"eliminating the social conditions closely associated with crime." "Riots must be suppressed promptly when they occur," the report went on, but what is needed is "a far more determined effort . . . to eradicate conditions that invite riots."[5]

But the Congress that passed the Omnibus Crime and Safe Streets Act of 1968 was meeting in the wake of the successive assassinations of John F. Kennedy, Malcolm X, Martin Luther King, Jr., and Robert F. Kennedy. The legislation was enacted against the background of the rise of black power, an increasingly militant anti-Vietnam war movement, and a growing national polarization epitomized in the presidential election of 1968, when Richard Nixon ran as a law and order candidate and aimed much of his fire at the civil libertarian values and policies of the Attorney General of the United States, Ramsey Clark, who had succeeded Katzenbach.

The volatile atmosphere of the time is captured in the remarks of Representative Edward Hutchinson (R. Mich.), who said, in a speech on the floor of the House on August 13, 1967:

> Mr. Chairman, it is unfortunate that we are called upon to debate this bill against the backdrop of violence. It is written to combat an increasing crime rate, not incipient insurrection.
>
> The return of sniper fire, the subjugation of rebellion, the quelling of mob violence enveloping large sections of our metropolitan areas, are tasks for the militia, not the police.
>
> Under the present circumstances, however, it is likely amendments may be offered to provide programs of improved riot training for municipal police and other measures prompted by events of the past two weeks and I would expect the House to adopt suitable amendments along these lines. Thus, the purpose of the legislation may be altered, or added to, as the House works its will. I think it should be pointed out, though, that the parts of this bill, as the House may amend it, motivated by riots rather than by crime, will be considered without sufficient evidence whether present riot training programs are adequate, what the states are already doing about riot training in municipal police forces, whether federal assistance is needed, and whether federal funds could be efficiently used.[6]

The Newark, New Jersey, disorders ended on the day the original House bill was reported out by the Judiciary Committee. A bloody riot in Detroit in which 43 persons were killed brought on a curfew that was lifted the day debate in the House began. The House accepted the Senate version of the bill the day after the assassination of Robert Kennedy in Los Angeles, and some observers mistakenly viewed final passage of the bill as a tribute to the late senator, who in fact opposed much of what the bill contained.

Most of the debate surrounding the passage of the legislation concentrated not so much on LEAA as on provisions to overturn the three recent Supreme Court decisions guaranteeing defendants' rights in the areas of confession, lineups, and searches and seizures, and to permit wiretapping in a wide variety of federal and state cases. So it is difficult to tell whether Congress thought it was creating LEAA to "reduce crime" or to "improve the criminal justice system" or both. The mood was decidedly one of cracking down on crime. As Congress stated in the preamble:

> To reduce and prevent crime and juvenile delinquency, and to insure the greater safety of the people, law enforcement and criminal justice efforts must be better coordinated, intensified and made more effective at all levels of Government.[7]

Presumably to further that objective, but also anticipating the Nixon era's mix of punitive jurisprudence and the New Federalism, Congress made four major changes in the Johnson administration's bill. Perhaps the most significant was the "Cahill Amendment." Under the administration bill, which was in the tradition of such federal programs as Old Age Assistance, Urban Renewal, and Aid to Families with Dependent Children, LEAA was to dispense categorical grants-in-aid directly to local and state governmental agencies.[8] The Cahill Amendment gave this function to the SPAs, which were to be under the authority of state governors. This change meant that the ultimate recipients of the money would apply to a state agency rather than to a federal agency for their funds. One of the motivations behind the amendment was disenchantment with Great Society programs, often run by "community people" over whom state officials had no control. Congressman Charles Sandman (R. N.J.) who spoke in support of the Cahill Amendment, referred specifically to an Office of Economic Opportunity–funded narcotics addiction center in New Jersey that had refused to follow the policy direction set by the state's Drug Study Commission; he observed that the result was two conflicting programs in one state. By providing for state agencies to dispense federal funds, he hoped to prevent such conflicts.[9]

A second major change worked by Congress probably had more to do with feelings about the civil libertarian values of Attorney General Clark than with political theory. Charles Rogovin, LEAA's first administrator, appointed by President Nixon, has written: "Despite his intelligence, humanity, fundamental decency and genuine concern for reform of criminal justice in the United States, Clark alienated many members of the Congress by his view of its needs and directions for a reform effort."[10] Congressmen feared, among other things, that the Attorney General might use the agency as a lever to force racial integration of local law enforcement agencies. In any case, the Senate placed control of the new agency in the hands of a three-person "troika" which, although it included members of both the Democratic and the Republican parties, was required to act in unanimity. The official rationale for the maneuver was that the LEAA, dealing as it did with local police forces, must be kept from the control of a single individual in order to prevent the establishment of a national police force.

The third change wrought by Congress was the creation of the National Institute of Law Enforcement and Criminal Justice, placed under the supervision of a director who could develop programs in his own office or enter into contracts with outside agencies for training and research to fight crime. (The original act would have placed criminal justice research responsibilities in a series of university-housed regional institutes.)

Finally, Congress added some special antiriot provisions to the legislation, giving grant requests for riot-control equipment top priority and allowing them to be funded by the Justice Department before the LEAA program was actually started and without their having to go through any state planning process.[11]

Thus was LEAA born in confusion and in reaction (in both senses of that word). President Johnson waited until the last day of the bill's active life to sign it (another day's delay would have resulted in a "pocket veto"); he then proceeded to implore Congress to repeal the "potentially dangerous" wiretapping section, which he said might intrude on the right to privacy of ordinary citizens.[12]

From the first, LEAA has experienced a brisk turnover among agency heads. President Johnson's choices for the troika—Patrick Murphy, former director of public safety in Washington, D. C., and police commissioner of New York City, and Wesley A. Pomeroy and Ralph Sui, his two associates—were never confirmed by the Senate, although they did administer a modest program for the remainder of the Johnson administration.

When Richard Nixon became President, he withdrew their names and nominated instead Charles Rogovin, a Democrat who had served on the President's Crime Commission, along with Richard Velde and Clarence Coster, two Republicans. Velde, the son of the late chairman of the House Un-American Activities Committee, was a staff aide to Senator Roman Hruska (R. Neb.), the powerful member of the Senate Judiciary Committee. Coster, a conservative former police chief from Bloomington, Indiana, was described by a colleague as having been "hardware oriented."*

Fifteen months later, in June 1970, Rogovin resigned, protesting that the troika was unworkable. He felt that LEAA had "failed to give policy leadership in the criminal-justice agencies it supports, and has therefore become a giant subsidy program, making little contribution to the improvement of criminal-justice administration in the nation."[13] He has since observed that "the basic flaw is in the mandate. Until the legislation is straightened out and you take out the idea that LEAA is going to reduce crime, you'll never get anywhere."

For the next 11 months until Rogovin was replaced, the agency tended to drift. But one component of the criminal justice system—the police—was organized to take advantage of the combination of a surplus of LEAA funds and a shortage of LEAA policy direction regarding how to spend those funds.

---

*Material within quotation marks for which no source is cited is taken from either interviews or confidential documents.

Rogovin has written that "too many police chiefs believed that the LEAA was a 'police program' to be run by them and for them and intended to address issues only as they perceived them."[14]

In May 1971, Jerris Leonard, unsuccessful Republican candidate for the U.S. Senate against the incumbent Gaylord Nelson (D. Wis.) and former head of the Justice Department's Civil Rights Division, was named administrator. By that time, the unanimity requirement had been removed, and Coster had resigned, although Velde had stayed on.

Leonard was the first administrator to give content to the agency's mandate, which was, as he saw it, "to reduce crime." With great fanfare, he announced the Impact Cities program, whose goal was to reduce a specific series of stranger-to-stranger crimes—homicide, rape, aggravated assault, robbery, and burglary—by 5 percent in two years and 20 percent in five years. Coincidental with Leonard's stewardship, the Uniform Crime Reports prepared by the FBI showed a drop in reported crime, and neither Leonard nor the Attorney General nor even the President wasted the opportunity to take credit for it. The LEAA-funded report by the National Conference of State Criminal Justice Planning Administrators, published in 1973, begins as follows:

> Crime in America was growing at an annual rate of more than 15 percent when Congress passed the Omnibus Crime Control and Safe Streets Act of 1968. Four years later the trend had been reversed and the nation recorded a 3 percent crime decrease—the first such reduction since 1955.[15]

When Leonard returned to private practice, he was succeeded by Donald Santarelli (April 1973–September 1974), another alumnus of the Justice Department, under whom the crime rate started to go back up, a direction from which it has yet to deviate. (It is up 18 percent this year.) Santarelli maintained that it had been a mistake to "sell" LEAA as a "crime reduction agency," since it should really be viewed as a "criminal justice improvement agency." Today, he says: "LEAA as a federal agency can't really reduce crime. It has no muscle to do it. Congress should take the words 'reduce crime' out of there."

The distinction between the goal of reducing crime and that of improving the criminal justice system may be a mere semantic quibble. But it also may reflect a profound difference in priorities and perspectives between the traditional, hardline, punitive law enforcement agenda and a more adventurous criminal justice strategy. The failure of both Congress and LEAA to resolve the question of mandate has resulted in confusion within and about the agency, in the formulation of conflicting criteria for resource allocation (hence, in a wasteful use of resources), and in abrupt policy shifts on the part of successive administrators.

In September 1974, after making some injudicious remarks about then-President Nixon, Santarelli resigned, and Richard Velde succeeded him. Velde's contribution to the debate about mandate is an assertion that the purpose of the agency is "to improve the criminal justice system for the purpose of reducing crime. And also with the basic understanding that the federal role is a very limited one."

The consequences of the failure of successive administrators to set LEAA on a constructive and consistent course have not gone unnoticed. In 1971, seeing that the police had received 66 percent of LEAA action money in its first year of operations while correctional institutions received only 10 percent, Congress passed legislation earmarking an amount equal to 20 percent of LEAA's action-fund budget to corrections.[16] The legislation directed the SPAs to establish a "comprehensive statewide program" for "construction, acquisition and renovation of correctional institutions"[17] and called for emphasis on such "advanced techniques" as community-based facilities, halfway houses, and supervisory relief programs.[18] In passing this legislation, Congress qualified its commitment to the block grant idea that states should set their own priorities. The original legislation had stipulated that "states and localities [were] to develop and adopt comprehensive plans based on their own evaluation of state and local problems."[19] But in earmarking funds for corrections, Congress was substituting its own priority for that of the states.

In 1974, upset that a larger proportion of LEAA's appropriations was not going to juvenile justice, Congress passed a Juvenile Justice Act,[20] which set up an entire administrative structure within LEAA and required states receiving federal assistance to agree, for example, "that juveniles who are charged with or who have committed offenses that would not be criminal if committed by an adult shall not be placed in juvenile detention or correctional facilities, but must be placed in shelter facilities."[21]

Not surprisingly, this year Congress has before it a bill called the State Courts Improvement Act, which would create a 20 percent category for court grants and would require the "court of last resort" in each state to do the comprehensive planning for the judiciary.[22] The Center for State Courts has deluged Congress with facts and figures demonstrating conclusively that the courts have been underfunded. Prosecutors and other groups also are likely to lobby for a piece of the pie.

●　　　●　　　●

The Law Enforcement Assistance Administration was conceived as a categorical grant-in-aid program by liberal Democrats living in the penumbra of a social philosophy that says that the primary cause of crime is the underlying social conditions that breed criminals. The legislation that created LEAA was passed by riot-scared, states' rights Democrats and Republicans anticipating the more punitive jurisprudence of the Nixon-Agnew era. The agency has been presided over by a rapid succession of administrators, each announcing new priorities and each leaving before he has had to confront the matter of mandate. As it appears today, even if LEAA is able to clarify its goals, the delivery system fashioned to achieve them may have been seriously compromised by Congress.

Because the block grant system was in part a reaction against "federal bureaucrats telling us what to do," it would be inappropriate to look to the Washington headquarters of LEAA for the sort of policy leadership that has been expected from categorical grant-in-aid programs (even those with built-in community participation, such as HUD's Model Cities Program or OEO's War on Poverty). But LEAA directly controls one-third of its budget (15 percent of its Part C funds as well as various percentages of the funds earmarked for corrections and juvenile justice, plus extra money that reverts to the agency from states unable to spend their allotted share), and it cannot help but make policy through the way in which it invests these funds.[1]

In the course of LEAA's first seven years, administrators have tended to publicize shifts in agency policy by announcing new programs. Four such programs are considered below. Although not all of them were of the same dollar magnitude, in each case the LEAA administrator, the public information office, and the monthly bulletin singled them out for extra publicity and attention as expressions of basic LEAA policy direction.

As a group, the programs—presented here in roughly chronological order—do not seem to reflect the orderly evolution of criminal justice policy. But the evidence suggests that personal, political, and, to a lesser degree, bureaucratic imperatives may have operated to subvert whatever the original policy thrust of the programs might have been.

Future historians will have to determine if LEAA's experience is unique or typical of the new federal programs of the 1960s and 1970s. But whether it can be ascribed to the block grant mechanism, the salience and volatility of the crime issue, the politicization of the Justice Department that characterized the early Nixon years, or all of these in combination, political interference has undeniably affected LEAA's programs.

The four national programs are Pilot Cities, High Impact Anti-Crime, Citizens' Initiative, and Career Criminals. These programs are not necessarily more noteworthy than other LEAA projects, such as the Standard and Goals project, the National Crime Panel survey reports (which assess the extent and character of criminal victimization in a variety of American cities), and statistical reports (*Expenditure and Employment in the Criminal Justice System*, for example), which have undoubtedly contributed to the nation's supply of criminal justice information. From another standpoint, LEAA may have made its greatest impact (at the national as well as at the state and local levels) through the police hardware, gadgetry, and advanced technology—including the massive network of information and communications systems—it has funded. But on balance, the four programs briefly described below seem representative of the interplay between the LEAA policymaking process and the underlying political process.

PILOT CITIES

In 1969, when LEAA was newly in operation, Robert Cushman, a staff member of the American Justice Institute in San Jose, California, submitted a proposal to the agency for a demonstration project; an action-oriented team of professionals experienced in criminal justice research would assist local officials in Santa Clara County "to identify and assess the dimensions of local criminal justice problems and then, by application of the most current knowledge and technology, help the officials to develop innovative programs for their police, courts, and corrections systems with the assistance of federal funds."[2]

The project would extend over five years and serve as a

sort of laboratory to develop, test, demonstrate, and disseminate new methods "for reducing crime in America." The unique feature of the project was its strategy, which would focus on jurisdictions and agencies—identified as "front-runners" or "champions for change"—that had the best possible environment, resources, and prospects to "show the way" to the rest of the country.

"Traditionally," says Cushman, "the criminal justice system concentrates the bulk of its resources on the offender who is most difficult to treat or in jurisdictions where crime reduction is often the most difficult." The design of the Santa Clara project was a conscious departure from that strategy. "We looked first for a county of about one million people with a core city of from 250,000 to 500,000 in population," he says.

> The idea was to find a jurisdiction with most of the common urban problems, yet small enough for a modest amount of money and effort to make some impact. It was important to find a well-managed jurisdiction, political stability, a toleration for research and evaluation and some sophistication in data processing. We looked for a community with demonstrated leadership and some success in addressing contemporary urban problems. We also looked for a jurisdiction with fairly well developed criminal justice agency services across the board so system improvement would not be forced to "start from scratch." We wanted to avoid having to spend a lot of time and resources helping a community establish the "basics," i.e. to bring services up to standard.[3]

Cushman's view was that there was no point in attempting a demonstration project in a county where it had no chance to succeed.

It took LEAA nine months to make up its mind, but ultimately, the agency decided to accept the idea. In fact, someone liked it so much that it became a program of the National Institute. (Richard Velde, the present LEAA administrator, who has been with the agency since its inception, recalls that the institute may have been toying with a similar idea before the Cushman proposal came in.) Either way, it was decided to try it not in one city but in three; then the number was escalated to seven, and the program was dubbed the Pilot Cities program. The seven cities were San Jose, California; Dayton, Ohio; Charlotte, North Carolina; Albuquerque, New Mexico; Norfolk, Virginia; Omaha, Nebraska; and Des Moines, Iowa. (Rochester, New York, an eighth city, was added late in the game.)

These cities received a total of $14.8 million in LEAA funds. In different cities, the money went for different projects. Overall (as of December 1973), 27 percent went for information systems and 23 percent for new types of community treatment services. Santa Clara built its Alcoholism and Detoxification and Rehabilitation Planning Center for $143,469. Dayton established its Target Hardening Task Force for $125,000. Albuquerque set up its five-man Metropolitan Narcotics Enforcement Unit for $65,710. Norfolk established its Chesapeake Police Minority Recruitment and Manpower Development Project for $43,313. Naturally, local needs varied, and the cities spent the money accordingly. As a result, Pilot Cities lacked the minimal degree of standardization necessary for what the original Cushman proposal described as "providing people with the ability to say 'another,' as it is now possible to talk about 'another' CYA Community Treatment Project or 'another' Provo experiment."[4]

In a memo from Gerald Caplan, director of the institute, to Richard Velde, administrator of LEAA, dated September 4, 1975, the "Findings of the Pilot Cities Evaluation" by the American Institute for Research are summarized. Was the program worth it?

> If the purpose of the Pilot Cities program was to reform criminal justice operations or to create model systems in eight middle-sized American cities, it failed. If, however, the purpose of the Pilot Cities program was to demonstrate that the Pilot team approach can work and work well under proper circumstances, it was a success.

The memo goes on to explain that the project failed by any criteria in five of the eight cities and that, of the remaining three, the most notable success was Santa Clara (which, of course, was the site originally proposed).

Three reasons may be given for Pilot Cities' problems. First, the program was tried in eight cities, although only one city—Santa Clara—was really ready to run a demonstration program. (Once such programs are announced, politicians scramble to get a piece of the action for their constituencies.)

Of the eight cities chosen, at least two—Omaha and Albuquerque—failed to meet the demonstration-city criteria set forth in the original Cushman proposal. But Omaha happens to sit in the home state of Senator Roman Hruska, the member of the Judiciary Committee who took the most interest in LEAA; Richard Velde, then a member of LEAA's governing troika, was his former staff man, and Hruska was and is generally regarded as LEAA's godfather in the Senate.

The other dubious city was Albuquerque. Today, Velde suggests that selection criteria "were not all that firm" and that Albuquerque, with the highest crime rate of any city in the country, "was chosen because we wanted one city with a very high crime rate." But according to a GAO report which evaluated the Pilot Cities program:

> LEAA documents show that Albuquerque and Tulsa were among the primary cities being considered as possible pilot cities in Region VI. National Institute staff visited the candidate cities and concluded that Tulsa best met LEAA's criteria and should be the pilot city. The staff rejected Albuquerque because it believed (1) the community's criminal justice leaders did not show much interest in the pilot city program, (2) the police chief appeared reluctant to implement innovative projects, and (3) friction between the police and courts on the one hand and the city and county managers on the other indicated an unstable political environment.[5]

The report says that Velde nevertheless told the institute to select Albuquerque and that, although the evidence was not conclusive, "New Mexico and Albuquerque officials, National Institute staff members, and LEAA Dallas regional office staff members indicated they believed Albuquerque was chosen primarily for political reasons."[6] The report does not mention that President Nixon chose the occasion of campaigning for a Republican senatorial candidate in New Mexico to announce the grant or that Senator Joseph M. Montoya (D. N.Mex.) tried to take credit for bringing millions in Pilot Cities funds to his state.

Another problem, referred to in the Caplan memo, arose from LEAA's policy of decentralization (which increased the power of the 10 federal regional offices of LEAA), adopted by Jerris Leonard in mid-1971. Under the new policy, the regional offices had the authority to approve or disapprove Pilot Cities' funding requests. Each of the seven LEAA offices eventually responsible for a Pilot City program adopted its own philosophy with regard to proper management. For some of the cities, this decentralization resulted in a drastic change of direction.[7] Thus, "although Dayton's phase I funding period expired in December 1971, the Chicago regional office did not approve its phase II funding request until May 1972 because the regional office was uncertain about the program objectives."[8] It is difficult to assess in absolute terms the benefits and damages resulting from this decentralization, but it is obvious that Pilot Cities was no longer developing as a national program.

Still another problem of the Pilot Cities program was that, before it was fully under way, LEAA developed and began vigorously promoting its new Impact Cities program, and a new LEAA administrator (Jerris Leonard) directed the regional offices to concentrate more on Impact Cities than on Pilot Cities.[9]

Thus did the politics of site selection and bureaucratic imperatives of regionalization combine with a new administrator's competing program priorities to undermine LEAA's first major demonstration program.

THE HIGH IMPACT ANTI-CRIME PROGRAM

The objective of the High Impact Anti-Crime Program— at \$160 million, LEAA's most expensive and ambitious effort—was aimed less at demonstrating anything than at reducing crime. Specifically, the Impact Cities program announced as its object the reduction of rape, homicide, robbery, assault, and burglary in eight cities by 5 percent in two years and by 20 percent in five years. Each city would get $20 million to do the job after its plans were approved by the relevant regional office.[10] The plans were supposed to be based on a crime-specific data analysis that each city would do for itself, prior to its funding of any projects.

The program was announced with much fanfare in the Indian Treaty Room of the old Executive Office Building in January of 1972 by Vice-President Agnew, with Attorney General Mitchell and Jerris Leonard at his side.[11] A few months later, Leonard told a group of SPA administrators, "We are finally on target as an agency. That target is crime."[12]

The cities selected were Atlanta, Georgia; Baltimore, Maryland; Cleveland, Ohio; Dallas, Texas; Denver, Colorado; Newark, New Jersey; Portland, Oregon; and St. Louis, Missouri. Impact Cities boasted two innovations. First, it provided each city with a model for what it called comprehensive Crime Oriented Planning Implementation and Evaluation (COPIE) intended to ensure (1) that the crime problems treated by the cities were indeed their major problems; (2) that the program plans reflected local priorities; and (3) that subsequent evaluation would tell them whether they had succeeded in reducing crime. Second, it called for each city to recruit a special Crime Analysis Team (CAT), an organization of researchers and functional specialists intended to coordinate all agencies involved in a city's Impact program. The idea was that the CAT team, working under an autonomous director, would prepare a master plan and an evaluation plan for the approval of the LEAA office in the region.

Martin Danziger, head of LEAA's Institute of Law Enforcement and Criminal Justice at the time Impact Cities was being organized, has given his version of the considerations that shaped the program.

To begin with, Danziger suggests that, not being a researcher, he acquired the National Institute job through a "fluke." He had begun his career in government as executive assistant to the special assistant for enforcement in the Treasury Department; later, he worked with an Organized Crime Programs Division at LEAA; when Jerris Leonard offered him a job as acting director of the institute, he agreed to take it only on the condition that he be considered in competition for the permanent job, which he got. As he describes it, "The National Institute was a potpourri of mudballs in the ocean. Grants were given to friends of friends. It was the classic grant system—incestuous. There were no goals, no system and no idea of the state of the art. No cohesiveness, but simply a list of projects." Danziger set out to change all that with a temporary moratorium on spending and a plan that included spending priorities. But he also set out to do something else.

At that time, the institute's budget was not what it might have been. Casting about for a way to expand his budget, Danziger decided to come up with a program specifically "to get control of the [LEAA] discretionary funds." He knew Leonard was interested in crime reduction; he wanted to get control of other people's money; and he wanted to "make a name" for the institute. The result was the Impact Cities program, which he remembers as being originally an idea for "research laboratories." (Richard Velde maintains that the program was not Danziger's idea at all.) At first, Danziger recommended three cities, but political pressures being what they are, the number was eventually upped to eight.

Danziger's criteria for selecting the cities included "high crime rates," "administrative viability," and "one-to-a-region." He claims that politics was not involved in the selection process, although, as in the case of Pilot Cities, there were rumors about how the cities were selected. In fact, Baltimore, Newark, and Atlanta used their first monies—prior to any planning or analysis—to put hundreds of new policemen on the payrolls, and the Impact Cities director for Newark was active in the mayor's election campaign. Such activities gave the program an aura of politics and patronage.

Where did the goals of reducing the specifically enumerated crimes by 5 percent in two years and 20 percent in five come from? "I just made them up. It sounded good." When asked recently whether setting goals like that doesn't invite failure and subsequent public disillusionment, Danziger replied: "No, it got attention and people are impressed with what you actually do. They needed the 20 percent goal for sex appeal. It was an educated guess and it was important to start setting quantified goals in the criminal justice system."

Now, three years later, the five-year program has been virtually abandoned. The administrators who followed Leonard have been unenthusiastic about Impact Cities. And although crime rates temporarily went down across the country (to date, no one has systematically compared rates in the eight participating cities with those in a control group), they soon went up again, prompting a chorus of sophisticated observations about $20 million not being enough to affect crime rates anyway.

The success or failure of Impact Cities is probably impossible to judge and certainly irrelevant to the question of LEAA policy. But six months after the program got under way, LEAA hired the MITRE Corporation, a research firm, to evaluate it. The MITRE report begins with the statement, "The issue in the evaluation of broad-aim programs is not, 'Does it work?' but 'What happened?'"[13] (This point of view is reasonable but inconsistent with the claims of the program's original advocates.) It is not MITRE's fault that the program was already under way before MITRE was retained, and by then it was too late to build rigorous evaluation designs into the program or to require area-specific or baseline data. MITRE's report, published in 1975, goes on to note:

> No control or comparison groups in non-impact cities could be envisaged for the national level evaluation due to the size of data-collection costs involved, no area-specific data collection within Impact cities could be undertaken for the same reason; and no presence was to be established by MITRE in the eight cities (it was felt by the National Institute that such a cost might be duplicative), such that national-level evaluation would depend entirely upon data . . . and information furnished entirely by the cities (by mail or over the telephone, for the most part).[14]

The MITRE report does attempt to track where the money went. Cleveland spent most of its money on high-risk youth offenders and emphasized community treatment and services. Baltimore spent most of its money on police projects, despite the fact that police were not listed as a city priority in the planning process. Over 60 percent of Atlanta's money went for police functions and target hardening. Newark spent 52.3 percent on police projects. As of September 30, 1974, Portland had spent only 18.8 percent of its Impact funds, most of it on corrections. In St. Louis, courts were listed as top priority but wound up with only 8.5 percent of the dollars. Only Denver appears to have spent money across the board in response to crime-specific problems. In fact, according to MITRE and most other students of the program, Denver was the most successful of the eight participating cities.

Some attribute its success primarily to the fact that, because city and county lines coincide, all of the relevant agencies are within one jurisdiction. But the Impact Cities program in Denver also benefited from the direction of Charles "Denny" Weller, a former policeman and parole officer with a Ph.D. in sociology, who is, by common consent, one of the most able criminal justice administrators in the country. He got the job through a competitive examination (few cities administer such an examination). And he began his work by recruiting a Crime Analysis and Planning team from all over the country, offering competitive salaries in order to attract top-notch talent. He then spent nine months collecting a baseline data bank that would enable his team to analyze the specific crimes and come up with a comprehensive plan. Before hiring any additional police in connection with the program, he had a special 40-hour training program in crime prevention developed for police use. Since Denver is a community with a high proportion of minorities, he set up his own equal employment opportunity requirements for every recipient of program funds long before LEAA itself adopted its less stringent regulations in this area. Unique among Impact Cities directors, Weller used no monies for the purchase of equipment (other than communications and information systems). And in advance of funding, he arranged for the state and city to pick up funding for the projects he helped organize so that they could survive after the LEAA money ran out.

The projects that Impact Cities in Denver initiated include a Community Health Program for Victim Support, a Rape Prevention program, a Community Outreach Probation Experiment, and a Special Crime Attack Team (SCAT), a project featuring flexible team policing designed to combat robbery and burglary in high-crime areas.

In the course of his work, Weller encountered—and overcame—two obstacles. First, LEAA's regional administrator did not want the program for Denver because it would involve extra paperwork and an administrative hassle (the other states in the region are predominantly rural). But the administration did want a program in the Rockies, and after some bureaucratic infighting, the regional office reluctantly went along. Second, Weller came under enormous pressure to get his projects going before he had finished determining what they ought to be. "There was all kinds of 'what's-taking-you-guys-so-long?' pressure on us," recalls Weller. "We were collecting our baseline data and they were telling us that in the first four months St. Louis has twenty-eight projects out on the streets and you guys have none!" What underlay this pressure was the presidential election of 1972 and an administration eager to get its money out on the streets before election day. "We didn't get our money out there until December because we didn't know where it should go until December," says Weller, but he ended up with 34 projects, a majority of which will survive the demise of Impact Cities.

Baltimore and Newark could not spend their share of the Impact Cities monies because they were too disorganized. In Baltimore, part of the problem stemmed from long-standing friction between the mayor's office and the police department (since the governor appoints the chief of police), which, among other things, prevented the Crime Analysis Team from gaining access to police data. In Newark, a history of corruption; the resentment felt by city councilmen of Italian origin toward the new black mayor, who appointed the director of the program; and a difference of opinion between the Crime Analysis Team and LEAA's regional office over the content of the program led to the resignation of the director and the dissipation of whatever enthusiasm the program might otherwise have inspired. (The CAT team charged LEAA with trying to impose a law and order flavor on a program that was designed to maximize community involvement; the LEAA office countered by claiming that the CAT team had not done its homework.)

The preliminary MITRE report attributes to specific Impact projects an astonishing variety of accomplishments. For example:

> St. Louis' Burglary Prevention Unit has achieved a 45 percent decrease in commercial burglaries. (The project involves surveying potential business targets, the installation of alarms, and business community education activities.) . . .[15]
>
> After Atlanta's Anti-Robbery/Burglary project had been in operation six months, the city-wide robbery rate had increased only 5% as compared to a 99.6 percent increase during the same time-period the previous year. (This project, which utilizes stake-outs, decoys and other tools of covert operation, has, however, been highly controversial in Atlanta and has run into serious management difficulties within the last year.) . . .[16]
>
> In 3 months, Cleveland's Pre-Sentence Investigation project reduced the average preparation time for all pre-sentence investigation reports to 7 days from an average of 21 days for jail cases, and an average of 42 days for bail cases. (The project involved the modification of the reporting form, and the hiring of additional manpower.) . . .[17]
>
> Clients of Denver's New Pride probation project, who have a history of recidivism and an average of 5.7 offenses per youth, had re-arrest rates, after one year of project operation, that were between 23 percent and 51 percent lower than baseline groups with equivalent numbers of prior offenses. (New Pride provides tutorial and cultural education, vocational training and part-time job placements to juvenile probationers.)[18]

But the data that MITRE offers to substantiate these claims are methodologically unconvincing, and despite all of the early talk about building evaluation into the program before permitting the dollars to go out, the MITRE report clearly demonstrates the impossibility of determining whether or not the program meets its original objectives. Nor does it consider the consequences of the program in terms of opportunities forgone because of the disproportionately large share of LEAA's discretionary monies committed to Impact Cities. The MITRE evaluation may serve public relations purposes, but it has not provided feedback to participating cities or generated the interchange among the separate cities that might have served to improve the programs as they went along. In fact, there is no evidence that the participants have paid any attention to it.

CITIZENS' INITIATIVE

The social programs spawned by the federal government in the 1960s did not succeed in eliminating slums or poverty. But Urban Renewal, the antipoverty program, and Model Cities did encourage the organization and participation of individuals at the local level who had previously been ignored in the decision-making process.[19] One of the early criticisms of LEAA was that it made no provision for citizen participation. Then, in April 1973, Donald Santarelli succeeded Jerris Leonard as LEAA administrator. In addition to trying to recapture some of the power Leonard had delegated to the regions and to emphasizing that the *real* purpose of the agency was not to reduce crime but to improve the criminal justice system, he proclaimed a new program. He said, "What we need is more citizen participation rather than more and more paid professionals." Shortly after his arrival, he made provisions to place citizens on state funding boards. He also inaugurated victimization surveys, a fresh approach to crime statistics, which dealt directly with private citizens rather than with crimes reported to the police. Their findings suggested a more alarming crime rate than that reflected in the Uniform Crime Reports prepared by the FBI. In January 1974, Santarelli created a Citizens' Initiative Office within LEAA's Office of National Priority Programs. According to the LEAA *Annual*

Report for that year, "This action represented the first formal recognition by a Federal agency concerned with law enforcement of the need to improve criminal justice service to citizens and to foster citizen participation in crime prevention efforts."[20] The motives behind this project were difficult to fathom. Santarelli, after all, was the man who had drafted the harsh D.C. Omnibus Crime Bill of 1970, which included preventive detention and "no knock" provisions.

The Citizens' Initiative Office prepared a brochure explaining the concepts behind the program and invited participation, inquiries, and project concept papers from "anyone interested in improving the criminal justice system in his or her jurisdiction."

"In fiscal year 1975," promised the *Annual Report*, "several million dollars in discretionary and block grant funds [a modest amount by LEAA standards] will be allocated to build citizen and community support for crime reduction and to make the criminal justice system more responsible to citizen needs."[21]

It was never a major program, but it attracted attention and stimulated some activity among old community activists. Alicia Christian of the Center for Community Change (now a staff member of the Black Caucus in the Congress) developed a proposal, in concert with a group of community organizations, which included BUILD in Buffalo, The Woodlawn Organization in Chicago, a Chicano group in Los Angeles, and a Philippino group in Newark. The idea was to set up a series of small storefront centers housing community-advocacy criminal justice groups that would engage in a substantive assessment of neighborhood security by means of tours; public hearings dealing with such issues as light and police coverage. The staffs would operate a 24-hour hot line, an escort service for the elderly, a "watch program" (a court-monitoring project), and other programs designed to build community awareness.

As with many such proposals, the group had to trudge from office to office, but on the fifth try, they ended up in the Office of Citizens' Initiative, where they were encouraged "to flesh it out." At this point, the National Urban League, the Center for Urban Ethnic Affairs, and a southwestern consortium of Chicano groups got on board, and before long, the group was told they would get a proposal number, although they would have to rewrite their proposal. In the LEAA bureaucracy, getting a proposal number is the next best thing to getting the grant itself; so, encouraged, the group went back to work, tailoring the project to LEAA's assorted requirements. In the midst of these negotiations, Santarelli made his public remarks criticizing the President and was forced to resign. With him went the enthusiasm for the Office of Citizens' Initiative. Six or seven go-arounds and 15 months later, LEAA was "still interested," but the project was unfunded. In December 1975, LEAA turned down the project on the grounds that the Citizens' Initiative monies had been diverted to another area.

As Leonard's departure signified the end of High Impact and its hundreds of millions, Santarelli's departure seems to have signified the end of Citizens' Initiative and its handful of millions. Of course, when a proposal is rejected by federal LEAA, its backers, theoretically, can apply in their home state for SPA block grant funds, but as E. E. Schattschneider pointed out over a decade ago, changing the locus of decision making means much more than simply altering the physical location of decision making; it may mean drastically altering the decision itself.[22]

As the arena of decision making is enlarged, Schattschneider argued, decisions favorable to the socially and politically disadvantaged are more likely to be reached; as the decision-making arena is decentralized, decisions tend to favor the status quo.

Schattschneider's thesis, if correct, is full of implications for LEAA's block grant system, and the available evidence suggests that grass-roots efforts of the type that Citizens' Initiative was meant to support are indeed less successful in dealing with the SPAs than with federal LEAA. Occasionally, a citizens group succeeds in navigating a grant through an SPA, but such successes are rare, the amounts small, and the processes painful. Recently, for example, a privately organized group of New Yorkers called Citizens' Inquiry on Parole and Criminal Justice, Inc., applied for a $20,000 grant from New York's SPA to research and write a booklet about probation in New York City. The grant was approved by the New York City agency; such approval generally means that approval by the New York State board will follow as a matter of course. But the day before the meeting, Diana Gordon, the director of Citizens' Inquiry, was told that "an upstate corrections organization" was objecting to the grant on the grounds that the Urban Coalition had produced a similar book. At the state board meeting, it turned out that the upstate corrections organization was the State Parole and Probation Officers' Association, which had circulated a memo to the board members describing the request for funding as "the wrong grant to the wrong group" because

1. It duplicated the efforts of the Urban Coalition.
2. Adequate information about probation was provided by the Department.
3. Citizens' Inquiry was incompetent and biased.
4. Probation might become wholly a state function in the future, and a publication about the city system would then become irrelevant.
5. The planning board's priority should be service, not publications.

When the grant came up at the meeting, the president of the Parole Officers' Association (the only outside speaker to address the meeting) repeated the charges in person. Gordon was given courtesy time to rebut the charges, which she had not been shown until 15 minutes before the meeting. By chance, the author of the Urban Coalition's pamphlet was also in the room; she agreed with Gordon that there was no overlap, and the grant was approved. "Well," says Gordon, "we got our $20,000. At least on paper. It will now take about three months to get checks sent to us. But it's now just about the only game in town, so I'm not in much of a position to complain." (The group has yet to obtain the money to print or distribute the booklet once it is produced.)

In September 1974, Richard Velde was appointed administrator of LEAA. He has had as his main areas of interest technology, the physical fitness of law enforcement officers, crime prevention through target hardening, and corrections. Plagued by internal dissension, he has yet to emerge as a strong policymaker, but he has shown himself to be a skillful bureaucratic infighter. A colleague says, "Talking to Velde is like playing ping-pong with someone who catches the ball."

At various times in recent months, Velde has announced grants totaling $4.2 million "to help prosecutors in metropolitan areas identify and quickly prosecute violent career criminals—those who habitually commit such serious crimes as murder, rape, aggravated assault, armed robbery and burglary."

The Career Criminal program was the particular brainchild of Charles Work, a deputy administrator of LEAA who was brought in by Santarelli and who has recently resigned, as part of a more general exodus of the old guard. He notes that "the career criminal generally has two or more cases pending in the court system at any given time." He observes that "the career criminal utilizes his familiarity with the criminal justice system to avoid prosecution and punishment. This program will break that cycle." The Career Criminal program has gotten a great deal of publicity, perhaps because the emphasis on habitual offenders is consistent with the views of the Attorney General and presumably with those of the President who named him. One day last August, the President and the Attorney General both took time off from their other duties to pose for pictures with LEAA officials and six prosecutors who had come to town to pick up the latest $2.3 million in grants.

The intellectual underpinnings of the program are set forth in the works of Harvard political scientist James Q. Wilson. In *Thinking About Crime*, Wilson points out that most serious crime is committed by repeaters and argues that what we do with first offenders is probably far less important than what we do with habitual offenders. A genuine first offender is in all likelihood a young person who will stop stealing when he gets older, but the habitual offender is someone whose incarceration may effectively reduce crime.[23] Gerald Caplan, director of the National Institute of Law Enforcement and Criminal Justice, keeps a stack of Wilson's books in his office and presumably distributes them to potential converts.

Velde apparently has a less jaundiced view of the possibilities of rehabilitation than has Wilson, and he appears to be less committed to the program than was Charles Work. However, given LEAA's sensitivity to the political climate, one assumes the program will last at least as long as Wilsonian jurisprudence is in vogue. (LEAA's propensity for responding to the latest trend is illustrated by a recent newsletter, which features a picture of the director of the National Institute chatting with the lead singer of the Beach Boys "about Transcendental Meditation and its possible use in crime prevention and rehabilitation programs."[24]) Of course, it is always an occasion for rejoicing when the current enthusiasm of a federal agency—hence, the availability of funds—coincides not only with the latest findings in the social sciences but also with the continuing concerns of state and local grantsmen. As one beneficiary of the Career Criminals program explained it, "I'm grateful for the money. I don't know what we'd do without it. But of course any prosecutor knows enough to spend his time going after repeaters—whether or not there is an LEAA program. You'd be insane not to. So to get the money, you call it a program." Undoubtedly, prosecutors need the money, but when they must juggle accounts, hire writers to prepare grant proposals, and pretend that a continuing function is a blue-ribbon experiment in order to get money, the entire criminal justice system suffers.

IV / *Current Operations: Other National Programs*

The Pilot Cities, High Impact Anti-Crime, Citizens' Initiative, and Career Criminals programs, taken together, show the effects of personality and bureaucratic variables on policy-making at LEAA. Four other national programs in progress also serve to illustrate LEAA's characteristic approach to criminal justice problems. These four programs implicitly reflect or have explicitly developed standards for the performance of various criminal justice functions. But LEAA has steadfastly refrained from insisting that state and local criminal justice agencies adopt these standards. A look at the programs suggests that the failure to require compliance with federal standards may be a policy choice that will have profound implications for our criminal justice system in the years ahead.

Two of the programs—the Law Enforcement Education Program (LEEP) and the National Institute of Law Enforcement and Criminal Justice—were mandated by Congress. The other two—the National Advisory Commission on Criminal Justice Standards and Goals and the nationwide funding of computerized crime information systems—were spontaneously generated by the agency.

THE LAW ENFORCEMENT EDUCATION PROGRAM

Section 406 of the Omnibus Crime Control Act authorizes LEAA "to carry out programs of academic assistance to improve and strengthen law enforcement and criminal justice." Under the law, LEAA makes payments to institutions *67* of higher learning so that they can in turn make loans (up to $2,200 per student) and grants (up to $400 a semester) to persons "employed in or preparing for employment in criminal justice agencies." In practice, some 90 percent of all LEEP participants have been "in service criminal justice personnel." Thus, although LEEP funds might have been used to train a generation of criminal justice planners, 80 percent of the LEEP participants have been police officers.

In 1969, the first year of operation, 485 colleges made grants to 20,602 students, and by 1974 (the last year for which figures are available), 95,000 students were receiving funds at 1,036 schools. LEEP's budget has grown as follows:

Funds Expended by LEEP

YEAR	STUDENTS	FUNDING (MILLIONS)
1969	20,602	$ 6.5
1970	43,000	18.0
1971	54,778	21.3
1972	87,000	29.0
1973	95,000	40.0
1974	100,000	44.0

Source: LEAA Annual Reports (Washington, D.C.: Government Printing Office).

Charles Rogovin had originally envisioned the program as involving the establishment of university "centers of excellence" at a small number of prestigious universities, which would develop strong curricula in "directly related" areas, but when he resigned as administrator in June 1970, the other two-thirds of the troika vetoed his proposal. In 1972, in accordance with the general policy of decentralization implemented by Jerris Leonard, responsibility for LEEP was delegated to the regional offices. Since then, school administrators have complained that policies vary from region to region and that new procedures keep being announced before the schools have had time to implement the old ones.

The law states that participating institutions must have

programs leading to a degree or certificate "in areas directly related to law enforcement and criminal justice." And LEAA has devised administrative criteria (size, location, program leading to criminal justice degree, etc.) for the selection of participating schools. In theory, institutions submit their curricula to LEEP for approval before receiving their allocation. Spurred by LEEP, a number of institutions have developed special curricula for law enforcement officers that are separate from the liberal arts curricula. But, in fact, LEEP has interpreted all of the behavioral sciences as falling within the program. If an institution teaches a course in one of the required areas, it gets the dollars because, in accordance with LEAA's policy of noninterference, LEEP makes no attempt at quality control of either course content or instruction. A GAO report describes the selection of participating schools as "subjective."[1] It might be more accurately described as chaotic. In 1971, nine people processed 900 applications in three days.[2] One former LEAA official maintains that Congress has permitted the program to develop in the helter-skelter way it has

> because 1,000 institutions qualify for those grants and loans—100,000 students. Every one of those guys [in Congress] wants some of that money for his district, so it's a very popular program. When LEAA finally got around to appointing a consortium to try to come up with a criminal justice curriculum, where did they go? To the centers of higher learning? Not at all. They went to Eastern Kentucky—it was strictly political.

But the numbers of people who sign up for the program attest to its popularity. The establishment of a program to send law enforcement personnel to college rather than to training programs conducted by the law enforcement agencies themselves reflects a recognition that the intellectual demands on criminal justice personnel cannot be met through job-specific training alone. But because LEAA is reluctant to impose quality standards on institutions that benefit from LEEP funds, LEEP students at Miami Dade Junior College, for instance, find themselves taking courses like Interrogation and Interview Techniques. Thus, what looks like a valuable opportunity for a rich education turns out too often to be mere police training.

THE NATIONAL INSTITUTE OF LAW ENFORCEMENT AND CRIMINAL JUSTICE

Under the law, the institute has eight main functions:

- To make research grants and contracts
- To undertake studies to improve and strengthen law enforcement
- To carry out behavioral research into the nature and causes of crime
- To make recommendations in the criminal justice field to federal, state, and local governments and law enforcement agencies for improving their operations
- To provide instructional assistance such as research fellowships and seminars
- To assist in conducting local, regional, or state training programs undertaken by LEAA
- To survey existing and future criminal justice personnel needs of the nation
- To report annually to the President and other related persons[3]

Although the institute accounts for only 5 percent of LEAA's budget, it has received much more than 5 percent of LEAA's press coverage, perhaps because its activities—ranging from a voice-print identification project to a study showing that Hispanics, largely because of language problems, are being denied equal justice—are the sorts of things that make news.

Like other parts of LEAA, the institute has changed its program and organization with changing personnel. In 1971, a task force report, commissioned by Jerris Leonard, declared that the institute's previous research program was "demonstrably unproductive." The institute then formulated a Program and Project plan emphasizing crime reduction. In 1972, it underwent fresh reorganization, including an effort to generate in-house research that would implement "research product utilization." Under the direction of Martin Danziger, it received more funds ($7.7 million) for its participation and leadership in the High Impact Anti-Crime program than it received for its entire budget the year before, and its total budget rose to $21 million. In 1973, Gerald Caplan, who had served on President Johnson's Crime Commission and had worked with Patrick Murphy at the Police Foundation, replaced Danziger. As part of his reorganization, he placed less emphasis on in-house research, upgraded evaluation projects, and inaugurated a series of new programs, including the National Criminal Justice Reference Service and the Exemplary Project-Prescriptive Package program, the purpose of which is to identify successful projects and to help communities set up their own projects based on these models. He also created the Office of Research Programs. The institute's budget is now $40 million, of which 27 percent is earmarked for advanced technology and 14 percent for evaluation. The chart below gives LEAA's own breakdown of how the monies are spent:

Distribution of National Institute Program Funds in FY 1974* (Listed by Program Area)

PROGRAM AREA	DOLLARS	PERCENTAGE
Community crime prevention	$ 3,483,160	10.7
Juvenile delinquency	1,707,768	5.2
Police	1,914,815	5.8
Courts	2,061,266	6.3
Corrections	2,547,019	7.2
Advanced technology	8,621,084	26.5
Education and manpower	1,274,550	3.9
Evaluation	4,414,005	13.6
Visiting Fellows	262,850	0.8
Technology transfer	6,355,884†	19.5
Total	$32,642,401	100.0

*Not including Pass Through Awards ($7,100,000 to the Drug Enforcement Administration and $1,225,500 to the LEAA Pilot Cities program) or purchase orders.
†This figure includes $4,544,988 in training and technical assistance funds.

Source: First Annual Report of the National Institute of Law Enforcement and Criminal Justice: Fiscal Year 1974 (Washington, D.C.: Government Printing Office, 1974), p. 50.

The LEAA administrator must approve all grants over $10,000, and friction between Caplan and Velde may help to account for the failure of the institute's grants to reflect any overall research strategy. Velde is partial to technical solutions for social problems, and his interests are reflected in such institute grants as

- $65,176 to Massachusetts General Hospital to study genetically determined variants in the structural proteins of human hair (to be used by crime laboratories to identify individuals)
- $508,084 to the U.S. Army Biomedical Laboratory to develop lightweight protective armaments for use by public officials and law enforcement personnel
- $80,000 to the Atomic Energy Commission–Brookhaven National Laboratory to demonstrate the feasibility of using sulfur hexafluoride as a taggant for the detection of explosives

One criminal justice researcher observes: "The trouble with the institute is that it has no research agenda. As a result, they get reports but not knowledge." Seven years of institute-sponsored research have failed to bring to light the basic causes of crime. One reason for this lack of progress may be that the institute has failed to establish research priorities. When, under Gerald Caplan, the institute finally attempted to do something about a research agenda, instead of canvassing the expertise presumably available at the SPAs across the country, it negotiated a contract with the National Academy of Science for this project. (The institute conducts no in-house research.)

Conversely, the institute has not insisted on having the findings of the research it sponsors applied at the state level. Although it presides over evaluation programs and a technology transfer program, the institute lacks the power and LEAA lacks the inclination to establish conditions whereby LEAA monies—even in the form of incentive grants—are used to replicate projects that seem to work, nor do they withhold monies from projects that experience elsewhere suggests are likely to fail. An indication of the politics at work in this area appears in the case of New York State's special prosecutor, Maurice Nadjari, whose office received over $1 million to investigate corruption. The agency mandated an evaluation of this project, but when Nadjari objected to letting the head of New York's SPA choose the evaluators and insisted on having veto power, LEAA "reluctantly" waived the evaluation.

A researcher would be hard pressed to demonstrate the institute's impact on the use of funds in the block grant program. One highly placed LEAA official comments: "The agency blew the ideal opportunity for a marriage between the Institute and the action program, when Velde, who views the block grant program as a form of revenue sharing, turned down the proposal to use block grant agencies to field test institute research."

THE NATIONAL ADVISORY COMMISSION ON CRIMINAL JUSTICE STANDARDS AND GOALS

Perhaps the major user of discretionary funds for an innovative project has been the National Advisory Commission on Criminal Justice Standards and Goals, which thus far has spent $1.75 million on producing, publishing, and disseminating its findings. The report on the findings, which was commissioned in October 1971, was announced by Jerris Leonard as "a new phase in the war against crime."[4] Twenty-two commission members accepted the job of putting together "a clear statement of national goals, performance standards and priorities, to translate as quickly as possible the billions of dollars that will be coming to states and local governments through LEAA into effective law enforcement."[5]

Like President Johnson's Crime Commission, the National Advisory Commission (chaired by Russell Peterson, a Republican, who was then governor of Delaware) was made up of reputable public law enforcement figures as well as a number of independent task forces on police, courts, and corrections.[6] The commission's efforts resulted in seven volumes. In May 1975, the LEAA newsletter announced an additional program to create standards and goals for new areas, including the private security industry. LEAA has provided $15 million to 42 states for programs, seminars, and meetings to set standards and goals and has distributed 30,000 copies of the volume on police and 21,000 of the other five volumes. (The Government Printing Office has sold 10,000 of each.)

When the report was released in 1973, Santarelli announced that it would make a major impact on the criminal justice system and on crime reduction and that it "is one of the greatest accomplishments of the Law Enforcement Assistance Administration in its first five years of operations. It will be one of the guides in determining LEAA policies and in evaluating the efficacy and effectiveness of its programs."[7]

At the time, Democrats suggested that the motivation behind the report was to give President Nixon his own Crime Commission. And it is true that the police volume, chaired and staffed by Chief Edward Davis of the Los Angeles Police Department, reflects the law and order orientation of the Nixon-Mitchell years. "Liberal" police chiefs such as Patrick Murphy were unrepresented on the commission, and not even enlightened centrist law enforcement figures such as James Vorenberg, who chaired President Johnson's Crime Commission, were consulted in the preparation of the report. The police volume ignores such matters as the need for minority recruitment but endorses surveillance spying techniques as "an essential tool of law enforcement"[8] and attributes part of the increase in the crime rate to the fact that "courts have applied more stringent standards for admitting evidence."[9]

The Standards and Goals publications, in general, go over a lot of ground already covered by President Johnson's Crime Commission, but they include some useful new material on victimless crimes (recommending the repeal of vagrancy laws and the reevaluation of laws on gambling, pornography, and prostitution) and on governmental corruption.

The key commission proposals in the various criminal justice areas include the following:

Police
- Consolidation of all police departments with fewer than 10 sworn officers
- Enhancement of the role of the patrolman
- Increased crime-prevention efforts by police working in and with the community
- Affirmative police action to divert public drunks and mental patients from the criminal justice system
- Increased employment and utilization of women, minorities, and civilians in police work
- Enactment of legislation authorizing police to obtain search warrants by telephone

Courts
- Trying of all cases within 60 days of arrest
- Requiring of judges to hold full days in court
- Unification within the state of all courts
- Allowance of only one review on appeal
- Elimination of plea bargaining
- Screening of all criminal cases coming to the attention of the prosecutor to determine if further processing is appropriate
- Diverting out of the system of all cases in which further processing by the prosecutor is not appropriate, based on such factors as the age of the individual, his psychological needs, the nature of the crime, and the availability of treatment programs
- Elimination of grand juries and arraignments

Corrections
- Restricting of construction of major state institutions for adult offenders
- Phasing out of all major juvenile-offender institutions
- Elimination of disparate sentencing practices
- Establishment of community-based correctional programs and facilities
- Unification of all correctional functions within the state

Criminal Code Reform and Revision
- Decriminalization of vagrancy and drunkenness

Handguns in American Society

- Elimination of importation, manufacture, sale, and private possession of handguns by January 1, 1983

Since the commission's findings have been published, critics have argued that LEAA ought to make some effort to have states adopt either the standards and goals of the commission or their own substitute standards and goals as part of the comprehensive plan. *"However, it is LEAA policy neither to endorse the Commission's specific recommendations nor mandate acceptance by states and units of local or general government of the Commission's recommendations."*[10]

Some state planners and grantees, nonetheless, copy Standards and Goals language in the documents they file with LEAA, but the report has not been the force for change that a more aggressive federal policy might have made it.

*THE COMPUTERIZED CRIME INFORMATION SYSTEMS**

In 1966, the President's Crime Commission recommended the use of computerized crime information systems by state and local law enforcement agencies. And in 1969, when LEAA went into operation, it made generous financial and technical assistance available to states and localities wishing to adopt such systems. At the same time, the FBI inaugurated its National Criminal Information Center (NCIC), a national repository of data that eventually became the basis of a computerized criminal history (CCH) program.

Although LEAA did not adequately address the policy issues implicit in its rapid funding of these systems, its actions were to raise profound policy questions, spelled out below. When LEAA began funding computerized information systems, only 10 states had such facilities. By 1971, 25 states had used LEAA funds to establish systems modeled on the

---

*The technical issues involved in the bureaucratic struggle among the various computer information systems have required us to compress much complex material into a limited space. The policy issues raised by computer technology are described in more general fashion on pp. 130–132.

NCIC and were able to draw on it for information regarding fugitives, missing persons, stolen cars, and stolen securities files.[11] By the end of 1972, 47 states had state-level criminal justice information systems,[12] and by 1974, all the states were covered.[13] By 1973, LEAA had spent over $50 million for this purpose, and in 1974, over 400 different systems were in operation at all levels of government.

In July 1969, LEAA designed Project SEARCH (System for Electronic Analysis and Retrieval of Criminal Histories). The agency's assumption was that few offenders are mobile on a national scale; since each state was to have its own NCIC-type system, what was needed was "regional systems interfaced between states rather than a national data bank."[14] The SEARCH system accordingly consisted of an "index" of criminal histories and a "switchboard" through which states could pass individual histories to one another upon request. It did not include a data bank.

At about the same time, LEAA began financing the conversion of the National Law Enforcement Telecommunications Systems (NLETS) from the primitive teletypewriters that had been used to a more modern computerized system. This law enforcement information system had been established in 1965 by a consortium of states, with each state financing its own participation. Ventures of this kind are highly compatible with the philosophy that underlies LEAA's block grants, and NLETS has received a substantial amount of LEAA funding—$2 million in 1974 alone.[15] Like SEARCH, NLETS has no storage capacity.

The FBI's NCIC, in contrast, retains complete files on individual subjects. These files are supposed to contain information solely on subjects of legitimate federal concern—violators of federal law and criminals with records in more than one state or with connections to organized or international crime.

Who should control the computerized criminal history data—LEAA or the FBI?

In 1971, over the objections of LEAA and the states, Attorney General John Mitchell placed the FBI in charge of the SEARCH computer system. In 1974, according to a source in the executive branch, Assistant Attorney General Glen Pomerening and FBI Director Clarence Kelly put pressure on Richard Velde not to approve a grant to NLETS. Without the grant, the state-based system would have been threatened with bankruptcy; ultimately, Velde did decide to approve the grant.

Recently, the FBI added switching equipment to its NCIC and petitioned the Attorney General for permission to begin using it. The White House Office of Telecommunications Policy allegedly responded by pointing out that the FBI's plan "would duplicate the existing capabilities of NLETS."[16] Attorney General Edward Levi has put off his decision on the FBI's request until Congress has the opportunity to consider it.

The FBI's attempt to take over the switching function may pose a serious threat to civil liberties. This equipment would permit the FBI to monitor all state-to-state communications. An officer in the White House Office of Telecommunications, in describing what he calls the "communication intelligence" activities of the FBI (the obtaining of information from the flow or occurrence of communication rather than from its content), cites "flagging" as an area subject to abuse. When, for example, a trooper in Montana makes a routine stop and runs an NCIC check on a motorist whom the FBI happens to be flagging, the FBI records the fact that the person has been stopped in Montana, even if the result of the trooper's inquiry is negative. (Obviously, this practice seems justified when it turns up fugitives who are subsequently convicted of crimes.) Recent correspondence between Senator John Tunney of California and Assistant Attorney General Harold Tyler has confirmed the fact that the FBI has used flagging to follow the movements of certain persons. Senator Tunney asked:

> Were flags ever used in the NCIC system for purposes other than to help locate persons with warrants outstanding, such as for allowing the FBI or other criminal justice agencies to know the locations of certain persons the agencies had an interest in? If so, please explain what such programs were and their duration.[17]

Tyler responded:

> Yes. Flags were used to help locate individuals in matters wherein the FBI had the obligation to determine their whereabouts in accordance with its investigative responsibilities in both the criminal and *national security* [author's italics] fields. . . . [S]uch flagging was done on a pilot basis from April, 1971, to February, 1974.[18]

Tyler responded more evasively to questions concerning whether state and local officials had known about flagging, who had contributed to the flag files, what the criteria were for placing a flag on a file, and whether any members of Congress had been flagged. Tunney phrased several of these questions in the present tense, and a few of them referred only to the NCIC system. Having stated, in response to an earlier question, that the practice of flagging had been terminated in the NCIC system, Tyler answered that "[t]he NCIC does not practice flagging" to each of these questions. If he had chosen to be fully responsive to Tunney's concerns, he could have stated that, for example, no congressman had ever been flagged, or he could have described whatever criteria had been used. His letter makes it clear that the FBI does use flagging in its manual systems, and the recent revelation that the FBI has maintained files on individuals whose only offense has been political disagreement with the administration suggests a reason for his evasiveness.

Of course, even manual systems of law enforcement record keeping can invade individuals' rights. But Aryeh Neier, executive director of the American Civil Liberties Union (ACLU), points out that the very existence of computerized information systems represents a temptation for the conscientious patrolman or state trooper to abuse it in order to check out suspicious-looking persons instantly through a local terminal at his headquarters or precinct house. Although such efforts only rarely result in arrests, the convenience and speed of the system may create an incentive for detaining and running checks on random suspicious people in the hope of turning up one who may have actually committed a crime.

Malcolm Barr, LEAA's public information director, reports receiving a letter from a doctor in a New England state requesting his LEAA "file." After referring the man to the FBI, Barr discovered the facts of the doctor's case. He had, apparently, been implicated in a kidnapping years before. He had been tried and exonerated, but that fact had not been entered in his file. As a result, whenever a kidnapping occurred near his home, he was picked up and questioned. According to Barr, the man's file still has not been corrected.

What safeguards are necessary to protect the civil liberties of those about whom information is maintained?

In 1970, the Standing Committee on Security and Privacy, which is connected with Project SEARCH, issued a report calling for specific safeguards to prevent violations of privacy and to preserve the integrity of the communications systems. The FBI found the report "very objectionable." A spokesman for the Justice Department, Jerome Daunt, said: "It is questionable . . . to suggest that a citizen has the right to inspect and challenge the content of Project SEARCH files. . . . I question the need for a 'code of ethics.'"[19]

After the FBI took over the operational functions of the SEARCH system, LEAA set up SEARCH Group, Inc., a research organization that deals with the issues of security and privacy. This organization is funded by LEAA, and its board of directors is composed of individuals appointed by state governors. Its representatives have testified at Senate hearings on privacy, and it has supported the concept of statewide computer information systems with nationwide switching capability (i.e., NLETS) as opposed to a national, centralized criminal information data bank (i.e., NCIC).

SEARCH Group, Inc.'s Standing Committee on Security and Privacy now consists of nine state representatives, a representative of the FBI, the general counsel to the President's Domestic Council Committee on the Right of Privacy, and an "LEAA monitor," Carol Deplan, who is LEAA's specialist for security and privacy. In October 1975, the committee issued a volume entitled *Standards for Security and Privacy of Criminal Justice Information.*[20]

Standards contains model state and federal legislation and follows the committee's previously published *Model State Act for Criminal Offender Record Information* and *Model Administrative Regulations for Criminal Offender Record Information.* The new volume differs from these two earlier documents in that it deals specifically with controls on both information *and systems* in a comprehensive way. It also addresses the NLETS/NCIC controversy and the deficiencies in present laws and regulations.

Standards recommends a national network modeled on the original Project SEARCH prototype: individual state systems with a central index to connect requests from one state to data sources in another. It also deals with the FBI's request to use its message-switching capability. The FBI argues that it can perform this function more efficiently than NLETS because it is already providing information directly to the state systems through NCIC, that adding "switching" would be simple and economical, and that a single federal agency would provide the most effective control over the use of the system. The advocates of NLETS argue that control of criminal justice information, like the operation of the criminal justice system in general, is traditionally and constitutionally a state function and should remain in the hands of the states. This argument reflects not only distrust of the FBI and the federal government but also the basic fear of a national police force that was evident in the debate surrounding the creation of LEAA. *Standards* recommends that, since the "'message-switching' question . . . involves important and highly sensitive issues of federal-state relations, . . . it should be resolved by the Congress,"[21] which is the branch of government best equipped to debate and reconcile these concerns.

In general, *Standards'* recommendations for the protection of privacy in state and local computer systems represent a thoroughgoing and largely successful effort to bring the legitimate concerns of the law enforcement community into harmony with those of civil libertarians.[22] On June 30, 1975,

LEAA issued proposed regulations and security and planning instructions for the use of states in preventing abuse of their computerized criminal information systems. Although, according to LEAA's general counsel, Thomas Madden, these regulations and instructions are for the most part consistent with SEARCH Group, Inc.'s *Standards*, a few differences are apparent.

Standards deals, for example, with intelligence information, an issue that has not arisen specifically in the context of LEAA but is a matter of public debate. Intelligence information is "information on identifiable individuals compiled in an effort to anticipate, prevent, or monitor possible criminal activity."[23] *Standards* points out that such efforts often generate information that is unverified, superfluous, and derogatory—precisely the kind of "raw" files that have been involved in recent revelations of abuse on the part of the FBI. *Standards* consistently imposes stricter criteria for the storage and dissemination of intelligence information than for criminal history or identification information and mandates periodic review for the purpose of purging such information from the files if no criminal prosecution is initiated against the subject. The LEAA regulations do not distinguish between intelligence and other forms of information.

Standards also addresses such situations as mistaken arrest, arrests not followed by prosecution, and misdemeanor and felony convictions followed by years of lawful behavior. The commentary explains:

> These paragraphs also recognize a public policy interest in permitting an individual's criminal record to be "forgotten" by society when he has indicated a strong likelihood of rehabilitation by staying out of trouble for a considerable number of years.[24]

Standards provides numerous guidelines for both purging (destroying) and sealing (making the records inactive but maintaining their physical existence and availability). The LEAA regulations take no stand on purging or sealing, leaving these matters to the jurisdiction of the states. On the subject of the individual's right to review and challenge his file, *Standards* recommends that the individual's attorney also be allowed to exercise this right. The importance of this issue becomes apparent in the cases of individuals who are unable to act in their own behalf—for example, while in jail. The LEAA regulations do not extend this right to attorneys.

Standards recommends that the challenge procedure include an administrative hearing; the LEAA regulations state only that LEAA grant recipients must permit individuals to review their records for the purpose of challenge.[25]

Standards recommends that no person should be required to transmit his file to another person; the purpose of this recommendation is to protect individuals from pressures by employers requesting their records for review. An LEAA spokesman has maintained that the agency's regulations and instructions to the states protect privacy in such instances by not requiring that an individual be given a copy of his record. Whether the absence of such a requirement would make it more difficult for individuals to obtain information from their records is not yet clear. The LEAA spokesman noted that the state procedures ought to provide, at least, an opportunity for the subject to *read* his record.

The regulations make no provisions for judicial review of official agency action, although, according to Thomas Madden, LEAA plans to recommend that the states provide both administrative and judicial review of challenges. Madden also points out that, under the proposed regulations, a local agency that refuses to correct factual errors would be subject to funding termination (which he concedes would probably not be invoked) and a $10,000 fine (which he considers a more likely penalty). In theory, LEAA can terminate the funding of a state that fails to abide by its own safeguards, but given the agency's usual reluctance to appear to be dictating policy to the states, LEAA seems no more likely to use this power to secure compliance with privacy and security regulations than to secure compliance with equal employment opportunity requirements, for example.

Of course, it would be unfair to maintain that LEAA has failed completely to exercise leadership in the area of computerization. In 1973, the agency established a Comprehensive Data System (CDS) program. To ensure that the various agencies reporting into these information systems would maintain readily available, uniform-quality information, transferable between jurisdictions, LEAA established guidelines (written by Project SEARCH) for analysis of data, updating, Uniform Criminal Histories, management and administrative statistics, technical assistance, and compilation of Uniform Crime Reports. To qualify for discretionary or technical assistance funds, each state must submit an "action plan" for the establishment of a CDS. By 1974, 32 states were participating in the CDS program. But this type of strong action on the part of the agency is rare, and thus far, situations that might call for termination of funding have not come to light.

One of the few issues in which LEAA's zeal for privacy and security appears to exceed that of SEARCH Group, Inc., involves the hardware to be used in the systems. The agency's regulations require that information systems be composed of "dedicated" hardware (equipment that is set aside for criminal justice use exclusively rather than shared, as many computer facilities are shared by commercial enterprises) and that access to such equipment be controlled and "secure." *Standards* argues against mandating dedication on the grounds that devices such as dedicated components and software packages can be used to maintain adequate security on "shared" systems and that the cost of computer equipment makes dedication economically unfeasible. A number of independent experts on computers and security also maintain that dedicated systems are unnecessary, but dedication is now the subject of a heated controversy between LEAA and state governors concerned about equipment costs.

In the area of computerized criminal justice information systems, LEAA has played an ambiguous role. Although it has funded the state systems, it also has resisted the FBI's efforts to centralize date collection and has funded SEARCH Group, Inc.'s efforts to promote safeguards for the systems.

The implications of the tendency of computer users to store as much information as the systems are capable of retaining have still not been fully explored. *Standards* represents a starting point for limiting the use of information contained in these systems, but only the public or its elected representatives can answer the policy questions the systems raise:

1. Is a national automated communications network between local systems desirable?
2. If so, who should administer it?
3. Should the FBI be allowed to perform certain communication functions for the states?
4. What safeguards are necessary to protect the civil liberties of those about whom information is maintained?

Until these questions are resolved, a moratorium on federal funding for both the purchase and the operation of computerized criminal justice information systems seems to be in order.

V / *The Block Grant at Work*

When the Omnibus Crime and Safe Streets Act, which created LEAA, was being drafted, critics had been attacking categorical aid programs for some time. They maintained that Washington was overly bureaucratic and given to devising universal rules that would have to be applied across the board to non-universal situations. The bureaucracy was stifling, the federal government was inflexible and out of touch, the paperwork was overwhelming, and the arm of the federal government was too long.

The block grant represented a halfway house between the old categorical grants and the New Federalism's program of general revenue sharing, a virtually unconditional aid program, both of which fund localities as well as states. (Over a five-year period ending December 31, 1976, general revenue sharing will have distributed $30.2 billion to 39,000 states, counties, cities, towns, townships, Indian tribes, and Alaskan native villages.[1]) It seemed easy to start with the field of criminal justice, since crime is a politically popular issue and is traditionally considered a state and local matter anyway. And it seemed logical to make the state the planning unit because only the state encompassed all three components of the criminal justice system (police, courts, and corrections), and only a state-level executive would have the clout necessary to get the traditionally fragmented elements of the criminal justice community cooperating with each other.

"Altogether," writes Richard Nathan, the Brookings scholar generally credited with being one of the founding

87

fathers of revenue sharing, "one can think of general revenue sharing and block grants as new forms of *broader* and *less conditional* federal aid programs for states and localities."[2] Block grants exist in four areas—community development, the Comprehensive Employment Training Act (CETA), social services (Title XX of the Social Security Act), and law enforcement (LEAA). But LEAA is the only block grant program that predates Nixon's New Federalism. The occasion of its extension for another five years (or its termination as of October 1, 1976) gives Congress the first opportunity it has had to see whether the block grant has worked, over time, as a delivery system. The question is whether the block grant, LEAA-style—which neither enforces standards and policy at the top nor allows states and localities to spend their money without going through the motions of comprehensive planning—represents the best or the worst of both worlds.

The three other block grant programs that are in any way comparable to LEAA are too different from one another to support generalizations about block grants in operation. And unlike LEAA, which essentially started from scratch, all three of the others were born as consolidations of previous categorical grant programs. The CETA program, for instance, represents the consolidation of 17 previous federal categorical grant programs (including Manpower Development and Training, Neighborhood Youth, etc.).

Under the CETA program, the key pass-through is not the state, as it is under LEAA, but rather a Prime Sponsor, which can be any city or county with a population of 100,000 or over. Prime Sponsors, like SPAs, have to submit plans for approval by regional officers in the Labor Department. But at the local level, the administrator can decide to continue each of the previous 17 categorical programs (although they are no longer mandated, having been officially eliminated by the legislation establishing CETA in late 1973).

There is a consensus among students of government policy that, although the federal presence in the block grant programs may be less than that in categorical grant programs, the size of the federal bureaucracy employed to keep track of the block grants is far greater than had been anticipated.

The LEAA block grants go to the SPAs. The size of the allocations is based strictly on population. In order to receive the grant, the SPA must file and LEAA must approve a comprehensive state plan for law enforcement.

STATEWIDE COMPREHENSIVE PLANNING

In the demanding words of the statute:

No plan shall be approved as comprehensive unless it establishes statewide priorities for the improvement and coordination of all aspects of law enforcement and criminal justice, and considers the relationships of activities carried out under this title to related activities being carried under other Federal programs, the general types of improvements to be made in the future, the effective utilization of arrangements between units of general local government, innovations and advanced techniques in the design of institutions and facilities, and advanced practices in the recruitment, organization, training and education of law enforcement personnel. It shall thoroughly address improved court and correctional programs and practices throughout the state.[3]

States are also required to provide one-quarter of the non-federal funding of local projects, and a mandatory pass-through provision requires that states allocate to local governments a portion of the block grant equal to the proportion of statewide law enforcement expenditures made by the local governments during the preceding year. Because the SPA generally approves these grants to local units on an individual basis, from the local perspective, the SPA is making categorical grants.

In theory, the planning process takes 12 to 15 months, and LEAA is supposed to accept or reject a plan in 90 days. The agency has 10 regional offices (Boston, Massachusetts; New York, New York; Philadelphia, Pennsylvania; Atlanta, Georgia; Chicago, Illinois; Dallas, Texas; Kansas City, Kansas;

Denver, Colorado; San Francisco, California; and Seattle, Washington) whose main business it is to review state plans for "comprehensiveness" and conformity to the guidelines. But they have seldom, if ever, accepted a plan on first submission, and they have seldom, if ever, ultimately withheld funding.

The agency issues guidelines for the SPA to use in preparing the plan. These guidelines, which run 200 pages in length, are a major source of friction between the SPAs and LEAA. The guidelines are revised annually, and they frequently arrive in the middle of a planning cycle; therefore, the SPAs often find that plans in preparation have to be scrapped. Some of the requirements in the guidelines result from the act and its amendments and concern such matters as the funding of high-crime areas, the composition of the supervisory boards, the awarding of applications within 90 days, the structure and contents of the plans, and state and local matching funds. Additional guideline requirements result from separate federal legislation, the provisions of which LEAA enforces, such as the Intergovernment Cooperation Act of 1968, the National Environmental Policy Act of 1968, the Clean Air and Federal Water Pollution Control Act, the National Historical Preservation Act of 1966, the Uniform Relocation Assistance and Real Property Acquisition Policy Act of 1970, the Freedom of Information Act, and the equal opportunity regulations of the Civil Rights Act of 1964.

Rather than terminate funding when a state's plan fails to conform to the guidelines, LEAA usually embarks upon grueling back-and-forth negotiations, revisions, and rewrites, and then attaches special conditions to the plan. Conditional approval means, in theory, that a state must comply with LEAA's requirement by a certain date or its funding will stop. In actuality, LEAA rarely checks up to see if the state has complied. Many SPAs seem to end up (if they can correctly interpret the complex federal guidelines) writing a plan that conforms to the guidelines rather than a plan that either reflects their own state and local needs and priorities or anticipates how the money will actually be spent. Only some SPAs turn in project-specific plans; most never mention projects in their plans.

Once the block grant is in the hands of the SPA, it is, depending on the state and the situation, parceled out either to recipient users directly or to substate regional or local planning units. Practices vary widely from state to state. Some SPAs literally make thousands of grants a year; others make only hundreds. Some SPA directors are responsible to the governor, others to a larger state agency. Some state legislatures have attempted to get involved in a direct way in the SPA funding process (asking for item veto power); others barely know that the SPA exists.

Although LEAA's experience does not provide a basis for systematic conclusions about the strengths and weaknesses of the block grant per se, observation of a number of states' LEAA programs does suggest answers to two basic questions: Has the LEAA block grant program successfully avoided the bureaucratic encumbrances that characterized the old categorical grants? And has it succeeded in stimulating statewide comprehensive criminal justice planning?

Of course, the presumption of many block grant supporters is that, even if the answer to these questions is no, a program that locates decision-making power at the state level is ipso facto more responsive and democratic than one that operates out of Washington.

THE QUESTION OF BUREAUCRACY

California is the one state that has made a study of LEAA's block grant program. Governor Edmund G. Brown, Jr., first focused on the LEAA program shortly after he took office in 1975, when a six-figure LEAA budget item for police protection of President Nixon's San Clemente home was brought to his attention. (Incidentally, LEAA funds were also allocated for police protection during the national political conventions in Miami in 1972.) The governor was looking around for a bureaucracy that he might attack to dramatize his new administration's frugality. As stories of massive LEAA boondoggles accumulated, he appointed a study commission to look into the whole enterprise.

The commission reported back that some 269 people were employed in administering the grant-review process at the state level and that their work involved "duplication of regional efforts as well as inordinate amounts of delay and confusion." The commission proposed delegation of decision making to substate units and recommended that the central SPA carry on its functions with a much smaller staff.

Governor Brown took the matter under advisement and finally (after calling LEAA a "pretzel factory") announced that he was going to put the program on trial. "If, at the end of the year," he said, "I'm not satisfied that this program serves the public interest, I'm going to very seriously consider returning the money to the federal government to help them fund their $80 billion deficit that they tell me will be created in the next fiscal year. Because I find it rather strange that this country can afford to spend money it doesn't have on projects that no one can understand."[4]

The governor's staff was then told that abrupt termination of the program might create legal complications in connection with ongoing projects and the commitments that had been made in anticipation of promised funding. Governor Brown also considered using the unspent LEAA money to employ youth in high-crime areas (California having 1 million unemployed) and/or to build jails. His staff put these proposals in a letter to Velde, who replied (via the regional office) that, since a comprehensive plan (prepared under the Reagan administration) for the expenditure of the fiscal year funds had already been approved, "funds must be expended by California in accordance with the plan."[5] If the governor wished to amend the plan, he would have to go through a series of procedures that were out of the question, given the commitments various localities had already made in reliance on the plan. Under the law, amendments to the California plan would have to be approved by the California Council on Criminal Justice (CCCJ), and the regional planning units in California would have to be given an opportunity to comment on any proposed amendments.

The letter from the regional office went on to say, "Many local government officials have contacted LEAA and have expressed concern that if the FY 1975 plan is substantially amended at this late date [May 15, 1975], they will be forced to lay off numerous people for lack of funds to pay their salaries." In addition, it was pointed out that California was already spending $3.4 million on LEAA-funded programs "with employment components" and that, if a planning grant were submitted by the end of the month, "over $10 million in FY 1976 Advance Action dollars can be available for the Governor's use on July 1 of this year." These funds could be used for employment "if the California Council on Criminal Justice amends the multi-year component of the FY 1975 Plan and approval is obtained from this office."

After sending the governor this letter, Velde paid him a personal visit to make sure he had gotten the message. The governor's assistant, Gray Davis, who later became chairman of CCCJ, then recommended that the state treat its subregions as autonomous and give them block grants to spend in accordance with their priorities, that the role of the central SPA be limited to quarterly policy meetings, and that the SPA staff be cut from 269 employees to 10. This recommendation, although satisfactory to the governor, was not regarded with favor at the federal regional LEAA office in California. In fact, the regional office staff told him that such a course of action was probably illegal because, as governor, he was required by law to see that the SPA did more things than 10 persons could handle. These tasks included developing and submitting a comprehensive statewide plan to LEAA annually, maintaining adequate financial management, supplying financial and technical assistance to the regions, ensuring that grant requests were processed within 90 days, providing for the control and acceptable disposition of property purchased with grant funds, employing a full-time civil rights compliance officer, and adhering to the requirements of the environmental protection act. This judgment was confirmed by a report issued by the Office of the Legislative Analyst of the state of California in August of 1975.

At about this time, the state of California submitted its annual plan. Although the federal guidelines for the preparation of state plans run to 200 pages, the plans themselves generally run twice that. Kentucky's 1976 plan ran around 2,000 pages. So the staff members in LEAA's Region IX office were somewhat startled when they received an advance copy of California's plan, which turned out to have a body of only 60 pages. (It also included a thick appendix containing the sub-state regional plans.) Shortly thereafter, Douglas Cunningham, the state's new planning director, arrived in the regional office, bearing the embarrassing news that, on the previous evening, the SPA had voted to defer the plan. He explained that a number of projects required further inspection before they could be ratified. For instance, Los Angeles County had applied for a grant of $2.5 million for 24 regional planning and evaluation units. Cunningham reported that the Brown administration suspected such units of being nothing more than "grantsmanship shops." (The Brown administration contends that, although Congress intended not more than 8 percent of the block grant to go for overhead, LEAA has for years permitted much more than 8 percent to be used for this purpose "under the guise of planning and evaluation.") Cunningham expressed disappointment that the LEAA regional office "had let this sort of thing go on." Cunningham further explained, somewhat sheepishly, that Governor Brown had performed the unprecedented feat of reading the plan, had been shocked at its length, and had ordered that it be cut back "to four or five pages." (Cunningham soothed those present by telling them that the original 60 pages would be added to the appendix.)

Subsequently, Velde has indicated that for fiscal 1977, two states, California and New York, "are going to have their plans turned back." (But as of this writing, both appear to have been funded.)

California is a special case, partly because Governor Brown has chosen to challenge "planning" (although he is not against "thinking ahead") and partly because he is using this particular program to dramatize the perils of bureaucracy. In the end, California's program may be no better, no worse, or not much different under Brown than under Reagan. But by taking the path of most resistance, Brown has exposed the double bind implicit in the block grant relationship: If the federal government follows a hands-off policy, it cannot impose and enforce standards. If it insists on and audits comprehensive planning, it cannot avoid setting up precisely the sort of bureaucracy that the block grant program was supposed to eliminate.

Complaints about bureaucratic impediments to action within the LEAA block grant system are not, of course, confined to California. Slade Gortin, attorney general of the state of Washington, has reported to the Senate Subcommittee on Criminal Laws and Procedure regarding the constant updating of the federal guidelines:

> For our 1976 plan, planning guideline manual M 4100-D was issued on March 21 and yet we had to have our completed plan to LEAA on September 30. This meant that all the planning tasks we initiated in January had to be modified, and sometimes reversed, in March so that we could comply with the September 30 submission date. Because the SPA is put in such a reactive situation, the cost of the planning process, with its many modifications, is more than it should be in dollars, time and sheer frustration. This kind of haphazard direction from the top turns an efficient state process into a haphazard one, too. . . .
>
> Our 1977 plan is due on June 30, 1976, but we haven't received the new guidelines. Our planning process must start NOW [October 8, 1975]! If the guidelines change radically we'll have a lot of problems and the usual grinding frustration. [These arrangements are forcing the state] into a horrendous six-month planning cycle instead of the year-long cycle we should have.[6]

The cities, of course, in addition to complaining that they do not get their fair share of LEAA monies, have long argued that the SPAs hinder rather than help their efforts to confront the crime problem. In testimony before the same Senate subcommittee, Mayor Harvey Sloane, M.D., of Louisville, Kentucky, spoke on behalf of the National League of

Cities, urging that Congress give block grants directly to the large urban areas. He invoked HUD's Community Development block grant program as evidence that Louisville and other cities have the capacity to provide for intensive planning and a coordinated, community-wide effort.

Sloane went on to describe the frustrations of the current system. "The present 'input' into the planning process for local governments," he said, "is at the bottom of a multi-layered system." Urban governments develop comprehensive criminal justice plans and submit them to the SPA. The SPA approves or disapproves, in whole or in part, a process that "in itself undoes whatever comprehensiveness there was in the local government plan, and provides in its stead a piecemeal package for localities."[7] The state comprehensive plan is then reviewed by the LEAA regional office and the national LEAA administration. The whole process takes months, and it encourages cities and counties to solicit funds for programs for which they know grants are available rather than for programs that meet a carefully planned predetermined need.

Wes Wise, the mayor of Dallas, has complained:

> We already have 1,311 pages of guidelines for a 23-page law. Certainly, if the Congress intended for state and local governments to have control over these block grant funds, to be able to develop priority programs, and to administer LEAA at the state and local level, then 57 pages of guidelines for each page of law will only frustrate, if not eliminate, our ability to accomplish these ends.[8]

The point is not that these officials oppose the program; they welcome the money. But this red tape seems as bad as, or even worse than, any encountered in the old categorical grants program. In fact, such testimony suggests that the program lacks the accountability of a categorical grant program on the one hand and the flexibility of revenue sharing on the other and that it is no more responsive to the will of the people than either alternative.

STATEWIDE COMPREHENSIVE PLANNING

Most observers agree that although LEAA has made a considerable contribution by bringing together representatives of the different components of the criminal justice system in "one room," very few states have really set in motion an adequate planning process. The Advisory Commission on Intergovernmental Relations (ACIR) has recently produced a preliminary and relatively sympathetic evaluation, but it states that "LEAA has been unwilling or unable to establish meaningful standards or criteria against which to determine and enforce state plan comprehensiveness and SPA effectiveness."[9]

Several reasons have been advanced for the failure of comprehensive statewide planning to take hold. In the first place, SPAs control only about 5 percent of a state's entire criminal justice budget and have no way to influence the elements of the system that are not financed by LEAA. Only Kentucky has given the SPA some sort of official planning jurisdiction over its total law enforcement budget, and even there, in practice, the SPA has not that much to say about how the money is spent.

Another problem is LEAA's guidelines, which are so complex and fluid that, instead of streamlining the planning process, they have reduced it to drudgery and irrelevance. As a result, many members of the state supervisory boards do not even bother to attend meetings at which planning is discussed. They come only to vote on project grants.

In the early years of LEAA, Congress observed that under the block grant system, the police were getting a disproportionate share of agency funds. The earmarking of special monies for courts, juvenile justice, and discretionary projects represented an attempt to make sure that these components of the criminal justice system would receive at least some LEAA funds. But the decision to earmark funds implied criticism of the block grant system, suggesting that the state was not the best judge of its own priorities. And in practice, as more of the money is earmarked by Congress, there is less room for the state to set its own priorities.

Finally, the tightening of state budgets has generated an atmosphere of economic emergency that is not congenial with systematic planning. Officials in the criminal justice system find it difficult to refrain from using LEAA funds to keep existing state programs alive. Moreover, in the absence of strong federal or state leadership, each of the components of the criminal justice system is more interested in getting its share of the pie than in sacrificing it for an abstraction, such as a comprehensive plan. The SPA meetings have become trading sessions at which, as one grant applicant puts it, "they sit around and vote money for each other." An unsuccessful nongovernmental applicant for a grant in New York has explained who "they" are:

> The law enforcement agencies make grants to themselves by having their boards represented on state and local planning boards. The preponderance of public agencies as grantees also demonstrates the cooptation in fact if not in spirit of outside groups. In New York at least a private group cannot get a grant from CJCC or DCJS [the state and city funding agencies] without endorsement of the relevant public agencies. And in fact the agency often submits the proposal and then subcontracts to the private group. This guarantees pretty effective control over the way the private group goes about its work after it gets the grants and what it puts in its work plan before the proposal is negotiated. It inhibits both innovation in and challenge to the sponsoring agencies.

The funding boards generally lack minority or community representation. The members give grants to each other's agencies in preference to "outsiders," and as one executive of a nonprofit institution tells it, the entry of LEAA on the scene may have coincided with the exit of other funding sources:

> Over and over it seems that foundations launch a good little project with "seed money" and then wean it after a

couple of years on the theory that if it's any good the big boys in the public funding arena will pick it up. Since that will only happen if the corrections commissioner or the police chief approves, the groups that are doing good work in pushing for change can't get continued funding. Good work on our terms is by definition not good work for the people we are turning to for funding and you can't blame them if their aim is to facilitate business as usual. So LEAA is really counterproductive to change and I can't believe the foundations don't know it but they don't seem to make the elementary distinction between funds available to cooperate and funds available to challenge.

The minutes of a meeting of New York State's funding body are illustrative of the results. The subject under discussion was a private group's proposal to bring citizen perspectives to bear on police problems:

Mayor Martinelli inquired whether this was not a normal police funding problem. By funding such groups as is proposed here, police departments are by-passed. The Chairman pointed out that in the Plan and federal statutes, citizen involvement is advised. Mayor Martinelli, agreeing with the Chairman, objected however to the funding of citizen group administration costs on the ground that the limited funds available could be better used. Mr. Cagliostro inquired whether Troy had tried but failed to establish a workable advisory committee and whether this proposal was required to bring such committee into being. He agreed with Mayor Martinelli and stated his opinion that the problem in Troy is one of government structure. Mr. Codd suggested looking at the possibility that the Troy Police Department be the applicant and responsible for setting up the committee in an existing agency rather than to have the committee set up as a potentially competing agency. Mr. Forman observed that the proposal was broader than only citizen-police relations. It is intended to raise citizen consciousness of the services that are rendered not only by police, but by courts, youth bureaus, probation departments, etc. . . .
Mr. Dominelli observed that the faculties of a number of colleges in Troy volunteer much time and effort and that, therefore, there is no need for paid administrators.

Judge Altman stated that New York City often works with volunteers but without professional staff, they don't produce too well. Mr. Grusky agreed indicating that Troy needs structure and a mechanism whereby to organize these efforts, to which Mayor Martinelli responded that the structure should be the police department; that this proposal sets up another agency working against, not with, the police department.

Mayor Martinelli made a motion that the proposal be rejected by the Board, which was seconded by Mr. Dominelli. On the motion, eight votes were cast to reject the proposal; six to approve it. The proposal, was rejected.[10]

The National Association of Regional Councils (NARC) recently sponsored a survey to determine the composition and membership of state criminal justice agency governing bodies. These planning groups define the types of projects and priorities of funding; they are pivotal in determining the nature and type of projects to be funded. A NARC spokesman, testifying before a Senate subcommittee, reported that

> [t]he preliminary results of the survey indicate that at least 17 states are not in compliance with LEAA Regulations concerning the representative character of state planning agency governing bodies. . . . Of thirty states where we have obtained information to date, thirteen state planning agency governing bodies had at least thirty percent local elected official representation. The remaining seventeen states had less than 30 percent and, in fact, four states had less than 15 percent local elected officials on the state planning agency governing bodies. These percentages are based on the LEAA more liberal definition of local elected officials which include elected law enforcement and judicial officers.[11]

County and city representatives frequently argue that the state is not the appropriate planning level. Charles Weller, the head of the Denver Impact Cities program, says, "I don't think planning can take place in a jurisdiction larger than a city. That's where the action is, and that's where the data is. If a planner is too removed he has little influence with the people whose cooperation he needs, and he doesn't know what's going on. The way it works now, the people closest to the data are furthest away from the agency that produces the planning document and we are not consulted."

The situation is not helped by the higher turnover in SPA directors. It is so rare for an SPA director to stay on the job that the professional association of criminal justice planners gives a special award to any director who has remained for more than five years. Florida, for instance, has had 19 directors in seven years.

Even where leadership at the state planning level is strong and effective, as, for instance, in Minnesota, which has had the same SPA director since 1969, the local government officials complain. John O'Sullivan runs the Criminal Justice Council in Hennepin County, in which 41 percent of the crime in that state is committed. He says:

At best our ability to influence the planning process is cosmetic. And it's not peculiar to Minnesota. The relationship between the local planning office and the SPA is a one-way street. This started as a forerunner to revenue sharing, but it has turned into a categorical state aid program. Either LEAA will die, or it will have to convert to a different system because the SPA is by definition isolated from 95 percent of the action going on in the state. Localities should be able to prepare their own plans and get money directly.

As a result of these tensions, the Hennepin Criminal Justice Council has discussed dropping out of LEAA and is seeking to become an organ of county government, where (1) it will be consulted in advance on its view of the priorities; (2) it will avoid what its members regard as unnecessary state-imposed red tape; and (3) it can move faster than Minnesota's annual funding cycle now permits.

Against these arguments, SPA supporters point out that police are organized locally, but courts and corrections are organized on a county and state level. Hence, the state is the only level at which comprehensive planning has a chance. According to Velde:

> Courts and corrections resources go beyond that of police functions of the big city. When you look at the problems of juveniles and addicts and alcoholics, cities are not particularly the people to do the planning and the managing there either. And they are very significant factors in the criminal justice system.

Robert Kane, the new SPA director in Massachusetts, points out that "if you gave the cities the money as revenue sharing, you'd lose the dynamics of the cities having to fight for and come up with solid research designs and careful evaluation to get the monies they use. You might get a situation where your innovative projects came to an end."

And Governor Michael Dukakis adds, "You have to have a mechanism for setting statewide priorities if you want to do more than just cut the pie up among the different agencies."

EVALUATION

The hallmark of an effective system, say the planners, is effective evaluation. In the early days of LEAA, a congressional investigation attributed major failures in program planning to the absence of a well-formulated plan for evaluation. It found:

- Although LEAA has authority under its enabling legislation to "conduct evaluation studies of the programs and activities assisted under the title," the agency has done little toward making its own evaluation of the effectiveness of programs or projects funded with block grant funds.
- Equally, if not more, important in terms of evaluating management performance and capabilities, neither LEAA nor State agencies which administer the programs have formulated standards for evaluating pro-

gram progress, success or failure. Thus, the programs are unevaluated, unaudited, and incapable of being measured as to performance and progress due to the lack of goals or standards.[12]

As a result of these recommendations, LEAA came up with its National Advisory Commission on Criminal Standards and Goals and undertook numerous reforms designed to build evaluation into the program. Just before he resigned as deputy administrator, Charles Work announced that

[the] state planning agencies are required to take into account the LEAA National Evaluation Program which seeks to create evaluation models. In addition, they must provide a mechanism for utilizing their own evaluations in planning future activities. Beginning in FY 1976, SPA's will be required to:

- Specify, in each program area, the source evaluation data consulted in developing proposed projects and programs.
- Describe how evaluation data has shaped the projects and programs included in the plan.
- Forward copies of all final evaluation reports to the LEAA Regional Office and the National Institute.[13]

But evaluation is not a panacea. A paper on evaluations in the criminal justice field, delivered at the 1975 annual meeting of the American Sociological Association, points out that "the mandate does not build in that only well qualified researchers will conduct these evaluations nor is cooperation on the part of the agency staff administering the program insured."[14] The authors of the paper attribute the dearth of what they call "efficacious evaluations" to three factors:

1. The agencies that fund criminal justice evaluations are not interested in efficacious studies but in success stories that will impress Congress favorably.
2. Even if the source of the funding wanted an honest job,

the administrators of the criminal justice programs (the SPAs or the project directors themselves) under evaluation might not share the same goal, and in 90 percent of the cases, it is these administrators who supply the data on which the evaluation is based.
3. Theories of criminology are too poorly developed to provide effective guidance for program design and usable criteria for evaluations.

In 1968, Robert Martinson, chairman of the Department of Sociology at the City College of New York, was approached by the New York State Governor's Special Committee on Criminal Offenders and was asked to undertake a survey of what was known about rehabilitation. The project, eventually taken over by New York's SPA, was based on the premise that the prisons of New York were not, at that time, making a serious effort at rehabilitation and that, depending on Martinson's findings, their function should be converted from a custodial to a rehabilitative one. By 1970, when the project was completed, the state had changed its mind about the worth and proper use of the information Martinson had gathered. As he recalls it:

> The Governor's Committee had begun by thinking that such information was a necessary basis for any reforms that might be undertaken; the State Planning Agency ended by viewing the study as a document whose disturbing conclusions posed a serious threat to the programs which in the meantime, they had determined to carry forward. By the spring of 1972, fully a year after I had reedited the study for final publication the state not only failed to publish it but had also refused to give me permission to publish it on my own.[15]

The case of Minnesota's Community Corrections program provides another example of the problems of methodology and politics in LEAA evaluations. Between 1969 and 1975, Minnesota's Governor's Commission on Crime Prevention and Control, which is Minnesota's SPA, awarded over $6 million to the Department of Corrections and to local units of government to establish and operate 40 residential community corrections projects throughout the state. The Minnesota commission, headed by Robert Crew, was in the forefront of the community corrections movement and took the view that LEAA's mandate was to test new approaches to criminal justice problems. "This purpose requires an objective evaluation of new programs to determine if Commission funds are achieving their hoped for results," said the recently released report on the program. This report, which runs to 370 pages, was published two-thirds of the way through the experiment. Its authors conceded that it was only "a preliminary evaluation and as such may raise more questions than it answers," but it tentatively answered a lot of questions, and most of the answers suggested that the program was ñot working.

The report revealed, for example, that only a minority of the clients

> successfully completed their programs. . . . Approximately 50 percent of the residents fail to complete the programs because they abscond, fail to cooperate with the program or engage in criminal activities. . . .
> There were only slight differences in the recidivism rates of clients who successfully or unsuccessfully complete half-way house programs. . . . There were no significant differences between recidivism rates of half-way clients and the comparison group in terms of arrest, felony convictions or total convictions and revocation of parole.[16]

This observation suggested to the evaluators that "residential community correction programs, for a variety of reasons, are an inappropriate form of rehabilitation for a large percentage of persons for whom these programs are now being used," that "the majority of persons sent to these programs are not amenable to the rehabilitation programs offered by the projects," and that, in terms of recidivism, the programs do no better or worse than traditional projects.

The report recommended that

[t]he Governor's Commission on Crime Prevention and Control should establish a moratorium on the funding of new residential community corrections programs. The sole exception to this moratorium should be those projects which test, under strict experimental controls, specific programmatic models. The Commission should determine if this moratorium is to take place within the awarding of 1975 funds or if it is to be placed in effect after the 1975 funding period.[17]

The evaluators insisted that their findings were tentative: "The evidence presented here does not mean that residential community corrections cannot be a viable concept. It is simply too early to tell. But the data do raise disturbing questions which must be answered before continuing unabated funding of these programs."[18]

As head of the commission, Crew received the report, accepted the recommendation of the evaluators, and ordered a moratorium on the funding of new residential community programs.

Within weeks, the Minnesota Department of Corrections staff responded to these actions by producing an evaluation of the evaluation, which conceded that the residential projects were not perfect and could benefit from the findings of "rigorous research," but they argued that

1. The evaluation research was "clearly of a preliminary nature."
2. It had been conducted on residential facilities of "limited scope."
3. The appropriateness of the definitions of "successful" and "unsuccessful" completion were at best open to serious question and at worst "misleading."
4. The research pointed out that clients could be diverted or released earlier with no jeopardy to the public safety.
5. "The methodology is open to serious question" due to lack of equivalence between the various groups, the

use of inappropriate statistical methods, and general poor sampling.

6. The reported underutilization of community residencies might well have been a function of "other elements of the criminal justice system which have nothing to do with the program."
7. The recommended moratorium on funding new residential programs "is not justified on the basis of the facts provided and will result in gross inequities for non-metropolitan counties."[19]

Here is one of the few programs in the country on which a serious and orderly evaluation was attempted, and the operational consequences of that evaluation are in serious dispute. Federal LEAA provided Minnesota with no direction whatsoever as to the procedures for conducting a useful evaluation. Possibly, despite all the talk, the priority is not to obtain quality evaluations but to involve the states in conducting evaluations so that Congress can be told that they are doing so. In any case, it is not clear that such LEAA projects lend themselves to serious evaluation.

Finally, as a pair of sociologists have noted:

It is important to recognize that all of evaluation research has an inherent conservative bias. We can only evaluate programs that exist and can only assess with confidence the range of parameters within existing programs. Alternative social programs that have been rejected for implementation cannot be evaluated and the effects of program characteristics beyond the range of variation within existing programs cannot be directly measured.[20]

THE USES OF BLOCK GRANT FUNDS

Given the constraints on evaluation, it may still be useful to know, if not how well, then at least *how* the block grant funds have been used. The LEAA *Annual Report* for fiscal 1974 breaks down the block grant figures into nine major categories:

Total FY 1974—$483,250,000

RANK	AMOUNT (MILLIONS)	PERCENTAGE
Detection, deterrence, and apprehension	156.26	32.5
Adjudication	66.85	13.8
Noninstitutional rehabilitation	59.65	12.4
Prevention	58.48	12.1
Institutional rehabilitation	46.85	4.7
Research and information systems	45.42	8.4
Diversion	30.33	6.3
Planning and evaluation	17.82	3.1
Legislation	1.59	.3

Source: Sixth Annual Report of LEAA (Washington, D.C.: Government Printing Office, 1974), p. 110.

But these figures do not indicate how much went to which component of the system or what is included within any given category.

A computer analysis of subgrants (block grant funds spent through the SPAs) done by LEAA's Grants Management Information System (GMIS) breaks the grants down into six categories: Police, Courts, Corrections, Combinations, Non-Criminal Justice Recipients, and Education (although education funds account for such a small percentage that they are not included in the charts). (See chart p. 109.) But the GMIS figures themselves are of questionable value. As a GMIS employee describes the "classification" process, when a grant comes in, a "coder" decides how to list it. But different coders list the same kinds of grants differently. An internal memorandum from a researcher at the National Center for State Courts refers to figures supplied by Richard Velde to Senator Burdick (D. N. Dak.) as covering expenditures for "purely courts" but indicates that the figures also include "alternatives to institutionalization," "community-based detention," "pre-trial detention," "investigating units," "youth services programs," "probation programs," and other noncourt functions.

The researcher also noted that the GMIS figures are generally incomplete, in part because LEAA does not require the states to participate in the program or to comply with fixed standards if they do volunteer to participate. The author of the memo had to go back to data for 1972 before he found a year with adequate figures, and even they turned out to be overly inclusive. In the course of seeking information in such categories as "police patrol," "automobiles," and "surveillance" (all listed in LEAA's key word catalogue), the authors of this paper were told that the numbers would be overlapping because the same grant was frequently listed in more than one category.

In February 1975, the Criminal Courts Techanical Assistance project, found that, although LEAA reported that the courts in four states (California, Georgia, Wisconsin, and Arizona) were receiving between 15 and 20 percent of the block money, the courts were, in fact, receiving only between 5 and 7 percent.[21]

Subgrants by Categories: Totals for All States

YEAR	NUMBER OF GRANTS	PERCENTAGE OF GRANTS	AMOUNT OF GRANTS	PERCENTAGE OF FUNDS
		POLICE		
1969	2,491	80	$ 15,353,220	66
1970	8,928	73	86,300,074	49
1971	10,118	64	140,074,594	39
1972	10,255	60	169,485,415	39
1973	8,047	55	180,993,491	39
1974	5,843	52	130,567,239	33
1975	1,193	50	36,532,533	40
Total	46,875	61	759,306,566	39
		COURTS		
1969	155	5	1,584,466	6
1970	969	7	11,336,793	6
1971	2,042	12	32,078,679	9
1972	2,740	16	60,566,043	13
1973	2,440	16	60,570,258	15
1974	1,968	17	61,994,173	16
1975	487	20	14,950,404	16
Total	10,801	14	243,080,816	13

Subgrants by Categories: Totals for All States (Continued)

YEAR	NUMBER OF GRANTS	PERCENTAGE OF GRANTS	AMOUNT OF GRANTS	PERCENTAGE OF FUNDS
		CORRECTIONS		
1969	205	6	2,450,103	10
1970	1,137	9	38,673,370	22
1971	2,105	13	106,945,646	30
1972	2,530	14	133,453,842	30
1973	2,252	15	142,412,258	30
1974	1,760	15	109,453,097	28
1975	356	15	24,187,152	26
Total	10,345	13	557,575,468	28
		COMBINATIONS		
1969	187	6	2,597,902	11
1970	836	6	27,856,544	15
1971	1,149	7	50,269,109	14
1972	472	2	29,288,972	6
1973	753	5	43,097,714	9
1974	767	6	49,051,426	12
1975	179	7	9,833,103	10
Total	4,343	5	211,994,770	11
		NON-CRIMINAL JUSTICE AGENCIES		
1969	53	1	1,113,157	4
1970	302	2	11,317,724	6
1971	493	3	23,932,866	6
1972	1,083	6	41,072,960	9
1973	932	6	34,072,747	7
1974	725	6	34,479,559	8
1975	128	5	4,755,997	5
Total	3,716	4	150,745,010	7

Source: LEAA computer printout.

The Advisory Commission on Intergovernmental Relations, in testimony before Congress, has used cautionary language about the utility of its own figures. These figures are based on a combination of GMIS statistics and surveys of SPAs, in which the state and local people involved provide data on themselves by mail and telephone—a methodologically suspect process, since people cannot be expected to provide unfavorable information about themselves. But the figures suggest, according to ACIR, a more balanced funding pattern than the one that used to characterize LEAA programs in at least two respects: (1) whereas the police used to receive over 60 percent of the funding, now their funding has "stabilized" at 40 percent, with corrections getting 23 percent and the courts 17 percent; and (2) high-crime areas are getting a higher share of the dollars than they either used to receive or would have been entitled to under a strict population formula.

The descriptions of the court grants listed on the GMIS computer printout were written by the grant recipients and are therefore of questionable accuracy. Time and again, pre-existing routine programs are given innovative-sounding project titles. As one student of the program says, "It's a shell game." This observation is confirmed by a rundown of the grants listed for two states chosen at random. Of Mississippi's 203 grants, 67 percent went for police-officer training or police-communication equipment in the form of small grants totaling $135,497. The University of Mississippi received a total of $504,681 in four grants, and the state Department of Youth Services received a total of $735,000 in a single grant. Ohio reported 106 grants, about half as many as Mississippi. Forty-three of these went to juvenile programs and 16 to enlightened rehabilitation programs. Ohio's grants also supported a course in Bushido and a program that provided bus transportation for families of prison inmates who wished to visit them. These figures are more a reflection of the inadequacy of LEAA's self-knowledge than an indication of what the states are in fact spending money on.

In response to detractors who dared LEAA to demonstrate that its $4.5 billion had been well spent, LEAA organized in 1974 Project Scheherazade, as it was informally known around the agency, and hired Abt Associates, Inc., to compile a list of 1,001 projects that had proved successful. According to one individual involved in the project, "originally, it was intended as the first part in a four-phase study. First, you identify the projects, second, you identify the variables in these projects which made them successful, third, you replicate the projects, and fourth, you test the replications."

With congressional reauthorization hearings around the corner, LEAA gave Abt only three months to conduct the first phase of the project. The Abt people devised four conditions and then sent out letters and got on the telephone asking for nominees. According to the conditions, the project had to (1) be in operation for at least one year; (2) significantly reduce crime or improve the operation or quality of the criminal justice system; (3) be cost effective; and (4) be adaptable to other jurisdictions. But Abt could only come up with 650 projects—out of all 85,000 projects LEAA had funded at that time. As a result, in June of 1975, the list of successes of Project Scheherazade became "A Compendium of Selected Criminal Justice Projects." The 700-page compendium purports to be "the first phase of a two-phase program to identify, evaluate, verify and eventually transfer promising LEAA funded projects." Among the 650 are the so-called exemplary projects, promising projects, and others, all of which were assembled by writing and phoning the various state, local, and national units and asking them to nominate projects that had worked and to tell why. The only editing LEAA did was at the bottom of each project description, in a section marked "Impact." Where the claim seemed to exceed the data, LEAA would add such lines as, "Procedures in selecting comparison group cases severely limit the confidence which can be attached to the difference [in the findings]" or "Since information on the dispositions of a comparable group of nonparticipating defendants is not available, it is not possible to judge the project's rehabilitative efficiency or cost effectiveness." A random sample undertaken for this paper found such qualifications in the description of well over one-third of the projects reported. When it appeared that LEAA was going to be refunded, however, plans for the next phase of Project Scheherazade were temporarily suspended.

It is, of course, impossible to determine what would have happened to the criminal justice system in the absence of LEAA. Richard Nathan, whose study of revenue sharing suggests that most revenue sharing dollars that are listed as being spent on law enforcement are really spent on other things. He recommends a similar study of what LEAA dollars are really spent on, but he speculates that, because they are allocated (at the state level) on a project basis, it is probably harder to divert them from law enforcement entirely.

The statute creating LEAA requires that state plans

> set forth policies and procedures designed to assure that Federal funds made available under this title *will be so used as not to supplant state or local funds* [author's italics], but to increase the amounts of such funds that would in the absence of such Federal funds be made available for law enforcement and criminal justice.[22]

A grant of $5,040 "to continue the salaries of two deputies of the Dillon County Sheriff's Department" in Dillon, South Carolina, may or may not meet these requirements. In the absence of an LEAA grant, the sum of $1,830 might still have been spent for "office equipment for the police department of Andrews, South Carolina." In a state like Minnesota, where the SPA operates on a 5-year planning cycle and makes only 135 grants a year, grants for things like police cars are prohibited. But literally tens of thousands of grants for cars, clothing, salaries, equipment, and such may be found in the computer printouts for other states which cover the latest fiscal year. Moreover, as more and more state budgets are cut back in response to the generally depressed economic conditions, LEAA money seems destined to continue to pick up rather than initiate a variety of criminal justice programs.

● ● ●

Because Richard Velde takes the block grant theory seriously (or perhaps simply because he is like most administrators), he maintains that his job is to get the money out, not to withhold it. As a result, he has never withheld money from a state for failing to come up with an adequate comprehensive plan or for failing to build in an adequate evaluation component. The regulations do not require LEAA to withhold money from a state for failure to attempt to implement the National Advisory Commission's standards and goals. As a matter of policy and legal interpretation, Velde has also chosen not to disqualify grant recipients on grounds of discrimination.

Nobody, not even Velde, denies that, if he did any or all of these things, he might run a tighter ship and have, at least for the foreseeable future, a more effective program. But as Richard Nathan points out, "If he did all these things it would be more interventionist than a categorical grant program."

VI / *The Issues*

When LEAA was about to be born, James Q. Wilson wrote that the billions of dollars the federal government was then preparing to spend on crime control would be wasted and, indeed, might even make matters worse if they were merely pumped into the existing criminal justice system. A few months ago, recalling his dour prophecy, he wrote, "They were and they have."[1]

The evidence is, on the surface, confusing. Richard N. Harris, chairman of the National Conference of State Criminal Justice Planning Administrators and an SPA director himself, can reel off lists of new things LEAA has helped fund in every component of the criminal justice system. For example, in the area of police service, he says:

> Many improvements have been made, from community relation units, training and education programs to crime laboratories, improved telecommunications networks and specialized patrol techniques. In Muskegon County, Mich. for example, our program funds have been responsible for that county's Centralized Police Dispatch System —it is a countywide four-frequency consolidated communications system which has reduced operational costs and allowed police officers to be reassigned to street duties. . . . [I]n Arkansas, we have funded that state's Law Enforcement Training Academy which has provided training to nearly 5500 officers in 184 courses and has utilized a mobile classroom in order to reach officers who

115

would otherwise be unable to take advantage of the program. . . . [I]n White Ridge, Colorado, police have created a special unit to help reduce commercial and residential burglaries.[2]

The district attorney of a county in New York State says: "Don't kill the goose that lays the golden egg. I don't know what I would do without it."

The head of a leading nonprofit criminal justice research institute that predated LEAA but now gets hundreds of thousands of dollars in LEAA grants says, "Whatever mistakes they might have made, because of LEAA there is more money around to do good things than there used to be."

Amos A. Reed, president of the Association of State Correctional Administrators, has testified:

> Frankly, the LEAA has been a near-godsend to state and local government, providing supplemental funding during the advent of a virtually continuous crisis situation in times of increasing pressure upon all portions of the criminal justice system. Without it quite frankly, we could have very little going for us in these troubled times. There is little doubt that many of America's correctional services would have been swamped long ago by the crime wave, had LEAA's backing and help not been available.[3]

Other observers are more critical. The radical opposition views LEAA as the forerunner of a national police force, generating SWAT squads, electronic surveillance, and the use of technology to subdue liberty. Scott Keating, director of Denver's Coalition Against Police Abuse, calls it "an attempt on the part of the government and those who control it to develop Big Brother tactics designed to intimidate left political people and instill fear in those people that are without the minimal essentials needed for a decent life."

Mae Churchill, of the Institute for Urban Studies at Loyola Marymount University in Los Angeles, California, believes that, by accident or by design, as a result of LEAA's funding of computer systems, the Justice Department will eventually have the capability of tracking every man, woman, and child in the country.

Those on the conservative side point out the lack of payoff from the $4.5 billion spent by LEAA. The crime rate is up (18 percent in 1975 alone), and the costs of the LEAA and the SPA bureaucracies are up with it. We know no more about the causes of crime than we did seven years ago, and we have not even perfected instruments to measure its incidence. Why not, these critics suggest, dump the money into general revenue sharing, and if the money is needed and wanted for criminal justice, let the localities put it there.

Despite, and to a degree because of, these varying assessments and prescriptions, a number of issues relating to LEAA's future have clearly been joined: first, issues having to do with the agency's purpose; second, issues having to do with the adequacy of the block grant delivery system (and the rest of LEAA's structure) to achieve that purpose; and third, issues having to do with fundamental democratic values (such as the rights to privacy and equal protection under the law), which, it is alleged, may be casualties of the LEAA program as currently conducted.

Of course, a prior issue is whether LEAA ought to have a future. Congress is right now considering whether or not to reauthorize LEAA for another five years. When the hearings before the Senate Judiciary Committee began, Senator Edward F. Kennedy expressed the hope that they would

> signal the beginning of a broad, comprehensive inquiry into the structure, methods and goals of LEAA. Such a comprehensive inquiry was denied the Senate when LEAA was reauthorized in 1973. At that time this Subcommittee held but two days of hearings; just three weeks thereafter the reauthorization bill cleared the full Judiciary Committee and reached the Senate floor for a vote.[4]

Thus far, the comprehensive inquiry Senator Kennedy hoped for in 1973 and again this year has not taken place, and it probably will not, given the domination of the Senate Judiciary

Committee by Senators Hruska, Eastland (D. Miss.), and McClellan (D. Ark.), all presold on the LEAA program. Although some witnesses have been critical, the sessions, for the most part, have been aptly characterized as "sweetheart" hearings.

The House Subcommittee on Crime Control is also holding hearings. Although it is less friendly to the agency than the Senate committee, the House subcommittee does not have the resources, the time, or the will to conduct the sort of searching, fact-finding inquiry that LEAA's $4.5 billion expenditure in the criminal justice arena demands. Without such a serious examination of this program, it would seem irresponsible to reauthorize the program for yet another five years. Perhaps a more prudent course would be to grant the program a year's extension while Congress does its homework. The administrative inconvenience suffered by LEAA programs and planners would be more than offset by the benefits of public dialogue and education that might accrue from such a congressional undertaking.

THE MANDATE

The original legislation establishing LEAA cites both reducing crime and improving the criminal justice system as objectives. In June 1973, the National Conference of State Criminal Justice Planning Administrators, an LEAA-funded organization that represents the views of the SPAs, issued a report called *State of the States on Crime and Justice*. The report begins by taking credit for the drop in the crime rate that had occurred in 1972:

> In 1968, Americans were twice as likely to become victims of crime as in 1960. Violent civil disorders in the cities, widespread drug abuse among the young, and a crime increase eleven times the population growth shocked and dismayed the nation. The traditional criminal justice system seemed unable to solve the problem or even to check its growth.

> The Omnibus Crime Control and Safe Streets Act . . . mandated a new intergovernmental and systemwide attack on crime through fifty-five State Planning Agencies (SPAs) representing both state and local governments. During the little more than four years since the SPAs accepted this responsibility, remarkable progress has been made. . . . The rampaging annual increase in crime has been halted and reversed. For the first time in seventeen years, crime has actually decreased. Moreover, during 1972, 94 of 154 cities (61 percent) with over 100,000 population reported actual crime decreases. In four years, therefore, crime in the United States has been reduced from an 11 percent increase to a 4 percent decrease and the number of large cities reporting actual crime decreases has gone from under twenty to almost one hundred.[5]

In October 1975, ACIR reported to Congress on its preliminary evaluation of LEAA, which is part of its continuing study of intergovernmental relations in the federal system. Its report included 10 case studies designed to demonstrate the experience of different states in administering LEAA's funds. Crime, of course, had gone up since 1973, and LEAA officials had dropped crime reduction as an agency priority:

> Most officials felt that the Safe Streets program should never have been expected to reduce crime and that the program has labored under unrealistic and unattainable expectations. They cite the small amount of funds in the Safe Streets program . . . the complex causes of crime, few of which can be affected by Safe Streets funds, and the necessarily reactive posture of law enforcement agencies as reasons why the program could not possibly have more than minimal effect on crime rates. . . .
>
> Many officials suggested that the Program may have led to an apparent increase in crime rates by increasing the level of crime reporting by the public and by supporting and encouraging improved record-keeping and crime reporting by police agencies.[6]

Supporters of LEAA have been reluctant to ask Congress to redefine the agency's mandate, for fear that, if Congress is told LEAA cannot do anything about the crime rate, it may not continue LEAA funding, at least at anything close to the present level. It seems hypocritical to insist that the purpose of the agency is to reduce crime, when virtually all expert testimony indicates that this is not a realistic goal. But the phrase "improving the criminal justice system" has been used by different people to mean different things. Donald Santarelli uses it to mean, mainly, reducing the opportunities for crime and increasing the risks associated with committing a crime; civil libertarians use it to mean, mainly, increasing the system's fairness, its humaneness, and its sensitivity to individual rights. A background paper prepared for a recent conference at Harvard listed eight objectives that the criminal justice system should pursue in addition to reducing crime: efficiency, safety of personnel, conformity with standards of due process, selection of the humane alternative, provision of social goods and services, acquisition of knowledge, citizen satisfaction, and citizen perception.[7] These objectives reflect a realistic, broad, and constructive perception of what government can and should do to further the national interest in this area.

Joseph L. White, former director of Ohio's SPA, has phrased the issue in terms of public policy:

> The Congressional interest in the quality of law, order and justice in America should be more positively focused on increasing the capability of the system to be efficient and humane and not demand, as a quid pro quo, a reduction in crime for every dollar. This should be so because we are a society which prizes efficiency and humanity.
>
> *New Rationale.* Congress should continue to express its concern about the quality of criminal justice for the same reasons that it justifies expenditures for other large social systems. It does not require the health field to eradicate cancer as a condition precedent to funding, nor does it require the educational system to maintain an intellectual level of excellence in America. It does so because those

services are the stuff of government, what the people want to collectively provide to themselves.[8]

LEAA might make a substantial contribution in the criminal justice arena by conducting and encouraging innovative research, experimentation, and evaluations as demonstration projects. The test of these projects, however, cannot be and should not be their impact on crime rates, and LEAA's mandate should be revised accordingly.

A conflict of interest is inevitable when criminal justice statistics are compiled by the agency whose performance is judged by them and whose funding is affected by them (as, for example, the Uniform Crime Reports are compiled by the FBI). LEAA could play a constructive role in helping to set up an independent bureau of criminal justice statistics, modeled after the Bureau of Labor Statistics. The initial promise and subsequent lack of follow-up on LEAA's own victimization surveys suggest the need for such a bureau.

THE BLOCK GRANT PROGRAM

The block grant program is under fire from those—mostly out-of-power Democrats—who would scrap it in favor of a federal grant-in-aid program and from those—mostly in-power mayors and other urban representatives—who would scrap it in favor of a revenue sharing program. The block grant system's supporters largely include those identified with state-level operations (many of the mayors who support it wanting direct-to-the-cities grants); they are also the chief beneficiaries of its largesse.

The arguments for categorical grants-in-aid and against block grants are much like those against revenue sharing in general—that national objectives are at stake; that national criteria should be brought to bear on the criminal justice system; that, in fact, there ought to be a national strategy, in other words, a national comprehensive criminal justice plan of the sort LEAA requires on the state level from the SPAs; that nationally raised funds should not be passed out to the states without more strings than LEAA is willing to attach; that the past ineffectuality of state and local governments in the face of crime is what caused the crisis in the first place; and that the poor, the minorities, the young, and the otherwise disenfranchised require the national government to use its leverage on their behalf against state and local establishments. On the other hand, Lieutenant W. Brannan, who heads the SCAT squad in Denver, says:

> I know there wouldn't be a SCAT squad if it weren't for LEAA, but I'll be glad when the money is gone because it's a pain in the butt. I'd much rather have the City Council fund us, which they are going to do. With LEAA you have to spend all your time capturing data for their monthly and quarterly and annual reports. . . .
>
> They selected three precincts with the highest rates of burglary. Our job [as part of the Impact Cities program] was to patrol them. The trouble was that one precinct was all the way over in a different part of town. That meant our men couldn't give each other support. They couldn't even operate on the same radio frequency. What we found was that burglaries, which were our target, went down substantially in the three precincts, but stick-ups went out of hand. I went to LEAA and said let us work stick-ups but there was a delay of three months before we were allowed to go after armed robberies. As a result, burglaries were down 38 percent in our target precincts but straight stick-ups and aggravated armed robbery increased citywide by 16 percent.

James Vorenberg was asked recently whether he still thought the old Crime Commission recommendation of a federal categorical aid program had validity. He answered:

> If I look back now at our thinking then, obviously we were informed by our own self-confidence. OLEA was spent well. We were smart guys who knew all the answers and seemed to be running things well, so categorical grants seemed the logical way to go. I still think if it had happened that way and we had been there it would

have worked. But if you are asking me am I sorry Richard Nixon and John Mitchell didn't have the billions of dollars to spend on a categorical basis? No, I'm not sorry.

The dilemma—federal direction versus local control—is as old as our federal system itself. But the attempt to straddle it with the block grant system, LEAA-style, has not yet been shown to work. *Either* a federal categorical grant-in-aid program *or* a general revenue sharing program (perhaps supplemented by a modest federal criminal justice institute) would seem preferable to the present mix, which lacks the benefits of either federal direction and priorities or local accountability.

As long as the block grant system is maintained, however, it should be structured in such a way that needy components of the criminal justice system are not frozen out of the granting process as, for example, the courts are alleged to be.

FUNDS FOR THE COURTS

The State Courts Improvement Act, recently proposed by Congressman Peter Rodino, would add a new section to the original act allocating for the use of the state courts an amount equal to 20 percent of the general action money. It would provide for comprehensive planning by the state's highest court or a body it designated and require the SPA to ratify the court's plan as long as it violated no fiscal accountability regulations. It also would require that 30 percent of the members of the SPA be selected by the governor from a list provided by the chief justice of the state. Half of the money would be provided in the block grant to the state, and half would be earmarked in discretionary funds for court use.

The National Conference of Chief Justices, which drafted the proposed legislation, argues that the planning process is, in fact, a political process, a point which has a number of implications for the courts. First, because they are weaker than police and corrections in terms of numbers and political clout, they get the smallest portion of funds. Second, it is unfitting for members of the judiciary to have to politick and trade-off quid pro quos in order to get a fair share of LEAA funds. Third, the need to submit their plans for approval by an executive agency conflicts with the doctrine of separation of powers.

Richard Velde has calculated that the courts get between 17 percent (1974) and 12 percent (1975) of the action funds. The GMIS figures suggest that the courts received 16 percent for 1975. But the analysis conducted by the National Center for State Courts indicates that LEAA's figures for courts include everything from prosecutors and defense attorneys to pretrial detention. The center's figures are probably more accurate than the LEAA figures, and the courts probably have been underfunded relative to other components of the criminal justice system. One way or another, something should be done to remedy that imbalance.

THE INSTITUTE

Although the institute has done some good things—it is proudest of its work on the relationship of architectural design to crime—its history has been a checkered one of low-quality research, the politicization of some of its programs, personality conflicts between director and administrator, abruptly changing priorities, an obsession with technology, and the lack of either an in-house research capacity or an overall research strategy.

Under Gerald Caplan, the institute has improved its procedures, but a recent grantee described its granting process as "still a caricature of peer review—essentially they ask two questions: 'Are you a good guy or a bad guy?' And 'will your project cause problems?'"

Under the proposed legislation amending the Omnibus Crime statute, the director of the institute would, in the future, be appointed by the Attorney General (rather than, as now, by the administrator), and his jurisdiction would be expanded to include civil as well as criminal matters.

A number of proposals have been advanced to help give the institute a clearer focus and to improve the quality of its work. For example, its evaluation program now draws heavily on former Defense Department research units ("casualties of the Vietnam war," one alumnus calls them) such as the MITRE Corporation. Instead of employing such "entrepreneurial" evaluators or allowing projects to evaluate themselves, the institute might attempt to structure more objective academic evaluation situations.

Another proposal calls for a long-range program to improve the institute's research and evaluation capacity. Under this program, the institute would devote a portion (25 percent) of its funds as seed capital to start small nonprofit, perhaps university-based, institutes around the country. Within five years, this effort should produce a diverse, decentralized network of criminal justice scholars and researchers throughout the country who could work under contract with the institute in the same way that Defense Department research spin-offs now do. (The assumption is that, after a predetermined time period, these institutes would be cut loose and operate or fail on their own.)

The granting process itself should be revised and perhaps modeled more closely on that of the National Institute of Mental Health (NIMH), which has been invoked by Gerald Caplan as a worthy standard. The NIMH system involves a number of units with specific areas of responsibility; a national advisory council made up of authorities who undertake final review of research projects and recommend their support or rejection to the director of NIMH; and "study sections," each composed of about 12 social and medical scientists who meet three or four times a year, review applications, provide evaluations, assign priorities, and sometimes even make site visits with the applicant-investigator. (Although NIMH procedures are imperfect, they at least provide a direction for the reform of LEAA's own practices.)

Some observers maintain that the institute should choose between basic research and applied research because the same organization should not attempt both. Given the pitiful state of the art of evaluation, the poor quality of most LEAA research designs, and the lack of knowledge about the causes of crime, one criminal justice researcher has suggested that the institute's budget be enlarged and that it become "like a giant Vera Institute," running a few meticulously designed, carefully evaluated major experiments on core criminal justice problems. Running such studies in, say, five states would generate the sort of comparative data that are needed and are not now available. Given the fact that the advent of LEAA has provided other potential sources of criminal justice research funding with an excuse for their own reluctance to support projects in this area, the institute may have a special obligation to encourage enough research of certain types through matching grants and other forms of collaboration with private funding sources.

In fact, encouraging innovation through experimentation, research, and evaluation is what LEAA should be all about. In the past, the institute, whose job it has been to do these things, has been cut off from the mainstream of LEAA's work and from contact with the block grant program. Operations like the Office of Technology Transfer exist mainly on paper. However it is structured, the institute ought to be deeply involved both in providing technical assistance to state and local criminal justice agencies and programs and in attempting to get at the basic causes of crime.

THE AGENCY AND DISCRIMINATION

At a time when statistics suggest that most violent crime is committed by and against blacks and other minority groups, fewer than 4 percent of all sworn law enforcement officers are members of minority groups and fewer than 2 percent are women.[9] A 1974 survey conducted by the Race Relations Information Center found that the only police department with an appreciable percentage of black officers was the Alabama State Highway Patrol (4.5 percent black), an agency under a federal court order since 1971 to hire more blacks.[10] More than 50 law enforcement agencies across the country have been found guilty of race or sex discrimination by federal courts in the past three years. But Winifred Dunton, the senior attorney in LEAA's civil rights office, speaks for the perspective of the agency when she says, "Our primary purpose is to improve the criminal justice system and reduce crime if possible. It is not to eliminate discrimination. That is important, but not our primary purpose."

Prior to 1973, the law was arguably unclear as to LEAA's duty. At first, the agency argued that Title VI of the 1964 Civil Rights Act, which forbids discrimination by recipients of federal money, did not apply to its program. Following criticism by the U.S. Commission on Civil Rights, which characterized LEAA as one of the worst federal agencies in regard to civil rights enforcement, the agency changed its position and, in late 1970, established an Office of Civil Rights Compliance. The office issued regulations that were criticized because they did not prohibit discrimination on the part of the supervisory boards of the SPAs or establish complaint procedures. Although eventually the office devised new regulations to remedy these defects, its staff remained too small (eight persons) to do very much.

In 1973, Congresswoman Barbara Jordan (D. Tex.) sponsored an amendment to the act—Section 518 (c)—which was passed. On the floor, she explained, "This amendment was *necessary to reverse* LEAA's traditional reliance on court proceedings to correct discrimination rather than undertaking administrative enforcement of civil rights requirements."[11] The amendment states:

> No person shall on the grounds of race, color, national origin or sex be excluded from participation in, be denied the benefits of, or be subjected to discrimination under any program or activity funded in whole or in part with funds made available under this title.[12]

The section provides that the administrator must notify the governor of the state when he determines that discrimination is being practiced by an agency under his jurisdiction, and he must allow the governor "reasonable time" to obtain voluntary compliance. If that does not work, "the Administrator shall exercise the powers and functions provided in Section 509 of this title."[13] Section 509 concerns the formal termination of funding procedure. Also the administrator is allowed *concurrently* to seek appropriate civil relief; to invoke Title VI; or, where there is a "pattern or practice" of discrimination, to turn the case over to the Justice Department to seek injunctive relief.[14]

As a result of the amendment, Richard Larson of the ACLU argues that "LEAA's statutory civil rights mandate is stronger than any other federal enforcement agency."[15] Most federal programs use the withholding or withdrawing of funds as a last-resort strategy, and most officials feel that, even as a last resort, such procedures are of dubious value because they alienate constituents, upset Congress, damage program goals, and can damage relations with the potential recipient of the funds whose goodwill may be an essential part of the program.[16] The main difference between LEAA and its civil rights critics centers on the question of whether or not the law requires the agency to stop paying money to discriminatory grantees. Dunton concedes that funds have never been terminated for civil rights reasons, although a number of letters have been sent to governors. The agency's civil rights regulations provide that "where the responsible department official determines that judicial proceedings . . . are as likely or more likely to result in compliance than administrative proceedings (i.e., funding termination), he shall invoke the judicial remedy rather than the administrative remedy."[17] She reports that, when the agency discovers discrimination, its policy is to seek judicial relief *rather* than to stop paying out the money. The civil rights community argues that this interpretation of Section 518 (c) is incorrect because the statute says "*shall* exercise the powers"—not *may* exercise. The agency's antidiscrimination procedures are currently the subject of a lawsuit filed by the National Black Police Association (NBPA) and 13 other plaintiffs.

Dunton finds the NBPA suit "very impatient." The civil rights office, she says "is doing quite a job" for its size. Its size, of course, is one of the issues, and it should be increased to enable the office to carry out its responsibilities.

In 1974, LEAA announced a new "enforcement strategy," requiring grantees who have more than 50 employees, who receive a grant of more than $25,000, or who are located in areas in which the minority population is more than 3 percent to prepare equal employment opportunity programs. To further this effort, a 250-page manual has been published, setting forth all the relevant laws, regulations, forms, and ideas.[18]

The grantee is not required to implement the equal employment opportunity plan, to file it with either LEAA or with the state SPAs, or even to show it to some government official. The recipient of the funds must simply file a certificate with the SPA, stating that he has an equal employment opportunity plan.

Richard Larson argues:

LEAA's negligence, or maybe wilfullness, in this regard cannot be excused for lack of precedent. [The Department of Health, Education and Welfare] HEW, for more than a decade, has required every school district in the country to file HEW-101 forms with its regional offices. This rather simple device has been used as the starting point for HEW's Title VI civil rights enforcement program.[19]

The agency does not actually discourage individual SPAs from taking more vigorous measures against discrimination. When Bob Crew, Minnesota's SPA director, let it be known that he would insist that all Minnesota grantees (including those with under 50 employees and those receiving less than $25,000) would be required to prepare an equal employment opportunity program, LEAA in Washington said that it would neither enforce nor object to such a requirement.

Recently, LEAA announced that it was beginning to pre-screen large grants (those over $750,000) made from Washington out of discretionary funds and that it has begun to attach special conditions regarding discrimination to certain grants; hence, in theory, if the recipient does not prepare a plan, the "fund flow" will stop. Thus far, out of LEAA's

105,000 grants, 23 have been "special conditioned" for civil rights reasons.

In October 1975, the Justice Department filed suit against the New Jersey state police (1,765 troopers, of whom 23 are black and 1 is female) and the Michigan state police (2,007 officers, of whom 25 are black and not one is female). Over the years, the LEAA arm of the Justice Department has given the New Jersey state police more than $8 million and the Michigan state police more than $10 million to support the very practices that the Civil Rights Division of the Justice Department now contends are discriminatory. This is not just another equal opportunity issue.

If LEAA were giving money to a clothing manufacturer, the issue might be less compelling. But LEAA is dealing with our national symbols of law and justice. In the past six years, LEAA has awarded more than $1.2 billion to law enforcement agencies. While supposedly funding reform, LEAA may be perpetuating racism.

COMMUNICATIONS SYSTEMS AND THE AGENCY

Since 1968, the number of states with computerized criminal justice information systems has grown from 10 to 50. According to its own 1974 *Annual Report*, "the LEAA program has provided the leadership, funds and coordination needed to create these systems."[20] LEAA has also taken the lead in connecting these computers in a high-speed national communications network.

The full implications of this funding were underexplored at the time it took place, and now an exhaustive technical, political, and legal analysis may be required to reveal what LEAA has wrought. Nevertheless, at least three issues merit immediate attention.

1. The agency has published for comment a set of regulations setting forth privacy and security guidelines, but it has not indicated what steps it will take to guarantee compliance.[21] Although LEAA has sponsored the development of safeguards for privacy in the collection and dissemination of arrest and conviction records, it has declined to make LEAA funding

contingent on adoption of these safeguards by state and local agencies, on the grounds that such a requirement would constitute federal interference inconsistent with the philosophy of the block grant. A determination must be made as to whether or not the theory of federalism justifies the escalating risk of privacy invasion. The nation now confronts the prospect of a centralized network of data banks with no systematically imposed privacy and security safeguards.

2. Who should control the national network of computerized criminal histories—the FBI, LEAA, or a third party?

Before LEAA came into existence, the FBI had a virtual monopoly in providing goods and services to local law enforcement agencies that could not afford them. Much of the FBI's power came from the fact that state and local police agencies were beholden to it. NCIC, which came into existence in 1967, has added to that power. LEAA, by funding a state-connected NLETS, has offered state and local law enforcement officials an alternative to the FBI's system and, as such, is regarded as a threat. The result has been a bureaucratic war over which system will govern. At least one student of the issue regards the struggle between LEAA and the FBI over who will control national criminal information telecommunications systems as a surrogate of the struggle between federalism and centralism.[22] The FBI would like either to get control of NLETS or to replace it. LEAA has been resisting.

Although computer technology is unquestionably bringing greater efficiency to the law enforcement community and to parts of the criminal justice system, the trade-off, in terms of potential and actual violations of privacy and individual rights, has yet to be determined.

3. In a recent speech, Richard Velde called for the establishment of "a comprehensive and interrelated information system that would include all components of the juvenile system—law enforcement, courts, detention, and corrections. Related areas involved in the prevention, detection and control of delinquents and diversion, treatment, and rehabilitation programs should be included."

Aryeh Neier, the ACLU's executive director, has testified that what Velde is proposing is a national data bank that would house, among other things, records on any child who may have gotten into trouble, is ever alleged to have been in trouble, or is thought by somebody to be the sort of person who might get in trouble in the future. He adds that "Mr. Velde makes the customary obeisance to the desirability of privacy and confidentiality and then blithely ignores all that is known about the ineffectuality of existing privacy protections."[23]

The law enforcement benefit of such a data bank must be weighed against the cost of stigmatizing large numbers of innocent people in the eyes of potential school administrators, employers, licensors, creditors, and insurers. Some observers have proposed establishment of a commission whose job would be to monitor the policies and practices of the computer network. Of course, such a body would have to be independent of whichever agency ultimately had control of these systems.

MONITORING LEAA

Funds supplied by LEAA were used in connection with security operations at the political conventions in Miami in 1972 and for the protection of Richard Nixon at San Clemente upon his resignation from the presidency. Politics has clearly affected such programs as Pilot Cities and Impact Cities. The state courts, in their plea for earmarked funds, have argued that obtaining grants from the SPAs inevitably involves them in a political process from which they should be exempt. Politics has affected project evaluations. And even the White House has, on occasion, intervened to secure and expedite a grant for a political ally. (The Nixon White House apparently intervened to supply Impact Cities funds for Philadelphia in order to get Mayor Rizzo's support in the 1972 election.) Nobody has made any sort of study of either the opportunities for or the actualities of political influence in the LEAA granting process at the state and local levels. It was recently reported that under pressure from Representative Peter Rodino, LEAA has continued to finance projects in Newark under the Impact Cities program, which its local director, Alan Zalkind, characterizes as a demonstration of "what not to do to reduce crime in the cities."[24]

The traditional method of insulating a federal agency against political impropriety involves some form of monitoring. But funds for independent monitoring projects are scarce. One logical source of monitors, the criminal justice research community, relies on LEAA for support. Those Washington interest groups that take a position on law enforcement issues are another pool of potential LEAA monitors. But since 1971, LEAA has provided at least $26 million to such groups:

National District Attorneys Association	$5,388,077
National Center for State Courts	5,341,909
American Bar Association	2,594,780
International Association for Chiefs of Police	2,398,750
National Sheriffs' Association	1,802,460
National Council on Crime and Delinquency	1,320,234
National Conference of State Criminal Justice Planning Administrators	1,303,795
National College of District Attorneys	1,082,441
National League of Cities	1,064,443
National Legal Aid and Defender Association	1,041,858
Council of State Governments	861,639
American Correctional Association	856,395
National Association of Attorneys General	442,990
International City Management Association	337,088
National Council of Juvenile Court Judges	221,849
National Association of Counties	178,733
National Governors' Conference	165,374
National Association of Pretrial Services Agencies	39,300

Civil liberties groups are missing from this list because most of them do not take money from the government.

Source: LEAA Annual Reports, 1971–74.

As a result, as one top LEAA official has remarked, "the relationship between the grantor and grantee is no longer at arm's length, and they no longer feel able to criticize us."

Perhaps a watchdog committee of distinguished private

citizens committed to an open society with libertarian safeguards for personal rights should be created to function as a sort of civilian board to review LEAA operations. Sarah Carey, the author of three reports on LEAA for the Lawyers' Committee on Civil Rights Under Law, has operated as a sort of Ralph Nader of criminal justice, identifying the agency's failings from a consumers' rights perspective. But as the agency moves from the expenditure of millions to the expenditure of billions in the highly explosive criminal justice arena, some sort of institutional check on our nation's fastest growing governmental institution seems warranted.

It was probably inevitable, given the political climate of the early 1970s, that the federal government's efforts to assist law enforcement would reflect the law and order philosophy and bureaucratic style that some—but not all—of LEAA's original advocates favored. But the federal government can justify playing a role in this sensitive area only if it goes beyond serving the immediate needs of the law enforcement community. The agency should be designed to serve the long-range aspirations of society at large in regard to criminal justice. For this purpose, representatives of the public who are not associated with the machinery of government or the passing fortunes of the administration in power are needed to participate in the decision making that determines LEAA's future. The federal government's war on crime is too important to leave to its generals.

Chapter I

[1]82 Stat. 197, as amended 84 Stat. 1881, as amended 87 Stat. 197, as amended 88 Stat. 1109. Title I of the Omnibus Crime Control and Safe Streets Act of 1968 is the enabling legislation for LEAA. It is codified at 42 U.S.C. Sec. 3701 et seq. All citations to the Omnibus Crime Control Act refer to the public law (P.L.) version appearing in the *Statutes at Large* (Stat.) and read "Title I, Section ______." Other statutes affecting LEAA are cited by name and section number.

[2]All budget figures appearing herein are taken from official published LEAA sources unless otherwise indicated.

[3]The items on this list are taken from an LEAA computer printout provided to the authors. See also, *Sixth Annual Report of LEAA* (Washington, D. C.: Government Printing Office, 1974), p. 177.

[4]To be comprehensive, Title I, Sec. 303 (a) requires that each state plan shall

1. Provide for administration of the grants by the SPAs
2. Provide for apportionment of the funds to local governments or combinations thereof, with the states providing 50 percent of the 10 percent matching funds in cash ("hard match")
3. Adequately account for local needs and local initiatives
4. Allow local units of government with populations over 250,000 to submit their own comprehensive plans to the SPA
5. Incorporate innovations and advanced techniques and contain a comprehensive outline of priorities for coordination and improvement of the criminal justice system
6. Provide for the efficient utilization of existing resources and encourage local units of government to combine and cooperate with respect to services, facilities, and equipment
7. Provide for research and development
8. Provide review procedures for those cases in which the SPA disapproves or terminates a local project
9. Demonstrate state willingness to assume costs of improvements funded after federal assistance ends

10. Demonstrate state willingness to contribute technical assistance to both state and local projects
11. Set forth policies and procedures that assure that federal funds increase the amount available and do not supplant state or local funds that would otherwise be spent
12. Provide fund accounting, audit monitoring, and evaluation to assure fiscal control and proper management
13. Provide for the maintenance of data and information for submission to the National Institute of Law Enforcement and Criminal Justice
14. Provide funding incentives to local governments that combine and coordinate law enforcement and criminal justice functions
15. Provide procedures that ensure that the SPA will approve or disapprove a grant application in 90 days, with reasons given in the case of disapproval

[5]The purposes for which action grants (both block and discretionary) can be made are set out in Title I, Sec. 301 (b) and are as follows:

1. Public protection through methods, devices, facilities, and equipment designed to improve and strengthen law enforcement and criminal justice and to reduce crime
2. Recruitment and training of law enforcement and criminal justice personnel
3. Public education relating to crime prevention
4. Construction of related facilities
5. Organization and training of special units to combat organized crime
6. Organization, training, and equipment for regular, special, and reserve units to deal with civil disorders
7. Recruitment and training of community service officers
8. Establishment of criminal justice coordinating councils in localities with populations greater than 250,000
9. Development and operation of community-based corrections and rehabilitation programs
10. Establishment of interstate regional planning units

The legislation includes a 10 percent matching requirement for federal funds (of which the state and the grantee must each provide 50 percent). Grants for construction must be matched with 50 percent nonfederal funds, and no more than one-third of any grant may be used to compensate police or regular criminal justice personnel. In some states, the SPA requires the grantee to pay a larger share of the match after the first year of the grant. The statute does not require the entire grant to be spent in one fiscal year.

[6]Testimony of Carl O. MacFarlane, on behalf of the National Association of Regional Councils, U. S., Congress, Senate, Judiciary Committee, Subcommittee on Criminal Laws and Procedures, Oct. 8, 1975.

[7]Title I, Sec. 401.

8Title I, Sec. 402 (b).

9Sarah Carey, *Law and Disorder* (Washington, D. C.: Lawyers' Committee for Civil Rights Under Law, 1973), vol. III, p. 9.

10U. S., Congress, House, Committee on Government Operations, *The Block Grant Programs of the Law Enforcement Assistance Administration*, 92nd Cong., 1st Sess., 1972.

11U. S., Office of Management and Budget, Issue Paper on LEAA, 1976 Budget, p. 20.

12Testimony of Chief Justice Howell Heflin, on behalf of the Conference of Chief Justices, U. S., Congress, Senate, Judiciary Committee, Subcommittee on Criminal Laws and Procedures, Oct. 22, 1975.

13Congress has superimposed legislation earmarking certain funds for certain purposes on LEAA's basic funding scheme. In 1971, Congress added Part E, which requires LEAA to allocate from its appropriation an amount equal to 20 percent of regular action funds (both block grant and discretionary) to be available for corrections programs. Fifty percent of the Part E money goes to the SPAs if they have submitted a comprehensive corrections plan with their regular annual comprehensive plan. The remaining 50 percent may be spent by the federal agency, according to its own discretion, for corrections programs. Part E contains an additional list of 12 requirements for a comprehensive corrections plan.

In 1974, Congress enacted the Juvenile Justice and Delinquency Prevention Act of 1974, which established an Office of Juvenile Justice and Delinquency Prevention within LEAA to administer a grant-making program in that area and which provided for state participation through the SPAs (with the inevitable requirement of a comprehensive plan in the area of juvenile justice). This legislation did not further subdivide LEAA's funds but provided, instead, for separate funding. Nor did the legislation establish a fixed ratio between block grant and discretionary funds. Congress was slow to fund the program, and consequently, the office was not established until June 1975. Its initial appropriations were $25 million for 1975 and $40 million for 1976.

14Testimony of Richard Harris, on behalf of the National Conference of State Criminal Justice Planning Administrators, U. S., Congress, Senate, Judiciary Committee, Subcommittee on Criminal Laws and Procedures, Oct. 8, 1975.

15Carey, *Law and Disorder* (Washington, D. C.: Lawyers' Committee for Civil Rights Under Law, June 1969; vol. II, Aug. 1970; vol. III, 1973). *Reducing Crime and Assuring Justice* (New York: Committee for Economic Development, June 1972.)

16U. S., Congress, House, Committee on Government Operations, *The Block Grant Programs of the Law Enforcement Assistance Administration*.

17U. S., Congress, House, Committee on the Judiciary, *Law Enforcement Assistance Administration*, 93rd Cong., 1st Sess., 1973.

18U. S., Congress, Senate, Judiciary Committee, Subcommittee on Criminal Laws and Procedures, *Hearings*, 95th Cong., 1st Sess., 1975.

19U. S., Office of Management and Budget, Justice Department, 1976 Budget, Issue #4, Law Enforcement Assistance Administration Budget Level (mimeographed); Justice Department, *Report Number 1 of the Department of Justice Task Force on the Law Enforcement Assistance Administration: Recommendations for Changes in the Legislation Reauthorizing the Law Enforcement Assistance Administration* (mimeographed), March 25, 1975.

[20]U. S. General Accounting Office reports, published by the Government Printing Office:

1. *Difficulties of Assessing Results of Law Enforcement Assistance Administration Projects to Reduce Crime*, B-171019, March 19, 1974.

2. *Federally Supported Attempts to Solve State and Local Court Problems: More Needs to Be Done*, B-171019, May 8, 1974.

3. *Long-Term Impact of Law Enforcement Assistance Grants Can Be Improved*, B-171019, Dec. 23, 1974.

4. *Progress in Determining Approaches Which Work in the Criminal Justice System*, B-171019, Oct. 21, 1974.

5. *The Pilot Cities Program Phaseout Needed Due to Limited National Benefits*, B-171019, Feb. 3, 1975.

6. *How Federal Efforts to Coordinate Programs to Mitigate Juvenile Delinquency Proved Ineffective*, B-168530, April 21, 1975.

7. *Federal Guidance Needed If Halfway Houses Are to Be a Viable Alternative to Prison*, B-171019, May 28, 1975.

8. *Problems in Administering Programs to Improve Law Enforcement Education*, B-171019, June 11, 1975.

[21]Sheldon Krantz, *The Right to Counsel: The Implementation of* Argersinger v. Hamlin (Cambridge, Mass.: Ballinger, 1976).

Chapter II

[1]Kennedy's efforts resulted in the conviction of 325 racketeers in his last year in office, as compared with 14 convictions in 1960. Robert F. Kennedy, *Pursuit of Justice*, ed. Robert Lowi (New York: Harper & Row, 1964), p. "Chronology."

[2]P.L. 89–197, 79 Stat. 828, the Law Enforcement Assistance Act of 1965.

[3]U. S., Congress, House, Committee on the Judiciary, *Anti-Crime Program 1967*, 90th Cong., 1st Sess., 1967, p. 86.

[4]Gerald C. Caplan, "Reflections on the Nationalization of Crime, 1964–1968," *Law and Social Order Law Review*, 583, 1973, p. 616.

[5]*The Challenge of Crime in a Free Society*, Report of the President's Commission on Law Enforcement and Administration of Justice (New York: Avon, 1968), p. 134.

[6]U. S., Congress, House, *Congressional Record*, 90th Cong., 1st Sess., Aug. 13, 1967, H9889.

[7]Title I, "Declaration and Purpose."

[8]U. S., Congress, H.R. 5037, and S. 917, 90th Cong., 1st Sess. (Same bills.)

[9]Statement of Charles Sandman (R. N.J.), U. S., Congress, House, *Congressional Record*, 90th Cong., 1st Sess., Aug. 8, 1967, H10072–3.

[10]Charles Rogovin, "The Genesis of the Law Enforcement Assistance Administration: A Personal Account," 5, *Columbia Human Rights Law Review*, 7, 1973, p. 12.

[11]Title I, Sec. 307.

[12]Richard Harris, *The Fear of Crime* (New York: Praeger, 1969), pp. 109–10.

[13]U. S., Congress, House, Committee on Government Operations, *The Block Grant Programs of the Law Enforcement Assistance Administration*, part 2, p. 464.

[14]Rogovin, op. cit., p. 23. A variety of other factors also contributed to the success of the police in gaining the lion's share of LEAA's funds. Among them:

1. LEAA's block grant applications were so complex that, in general, only those with a fair prospect of winning the grant bothered to apply.
2. The police community was overrepresented on the decision-making boards.
3. Since in the absence of clear granting criteria a lot of politicking was involved in the granting process, the courts were timid about jumping into the fray.
4. The LEAA-spawned hardware industry, which realized that it was able to increase its sales by offering to prepare LEAA grant applications, found ready customers in the police departments.
5. The matching requirements of the act skewed the process in favor of police departments, who could obtain matching funds more easily than could unofficial community groups of the sort who typically sponsor counseling and therapy programs for addicts, parolees, and juveniles.
6. The act's prohibition against spending more than one-third of any grant for the compensation of personnel turned out to work in favor of the police, who could always request funds for helicopters, communications equipment, automobiles, and other hardware, in contrast to community-based groups, courts, and corrections, whose innovative programs might depend primarily on people.

Although police funding has declined in recent years, the police still get a higher percentage of grants than any other component of the funding process. The table below, based on figures supplied from the LEAA's Grants Management Information System, shows that police projects have never represented less than 50 percent of the number of action grants. For the entire period from 1969 until August 1975, the police received 61 percent of all action grants.

Grants to Police Departments as a Percentage of All Action Grants

YEAR	NUMBER OF GRANTS	PERCENTAGE OF GRANTS	AMOUNT (MILLIONS)	PERCENTAGE OF ACTION FUND
1969	2,491	80	15.4	66
1970	8,928	73	86.3	49
1971	10,118	64	140.1	40
1972	10,255	60	169.5	42
1973	8,047	55	181.0	43
1974	5,843	52	130.6	36
1975*	1,193	50	36.0	43
Total	46,875	61	758.9	39

*Partial figures.

Source: LEAA computer printout.

See also, J. N. Varon, "A Reexamination of the Law Enforcement Assistance Administration," *Stanford Law Review*, 27, May 1975, p. 1303 ff.

[15]National Conference of State Criminal Justice Planning Administrators, *State of the States on Crime and Justice: An Analysis of State Administration of the Safe Streets Act* (Frankfort, Ky.: National Conference of State Criminal Justice Planning Administrators, June 1, 1973), p. ii.

[16]84 Stat. 1881. The Omnibus Crime Control Act of 1971 added Part E to Title I of the Omnibus Crime Control Act and Safe Streets Act of 1968.

[17]Title I, Part E, Sec. 453 (1).

[18]Title I, Part E, Sec. 453 (4).

[19]Title I, Sec. 201.

[20]The Juvenile Justice and Delinquency Prevention Act of 1974, P.L. 93–415, 88 Stat. 1109, codified at 42 U.S.C. 5601 et seq.

[21]Sec. 223 (a) (12) of the Juvenile Justice Act, 88 Stat. 1121, 42 U.S.C. 5633 (a) (12).

[22]U. S., Congress, House, H.R. 8967, 94th Cong., 1st Sess., submitted by Peter W. Rodino, Jr. (D. N.J.), by request, July 28, 1975.

Chapter III

[1]The agency also cannot help but exert some minor policy influence over the way in which the block grant money is spent through its power of ratifying state plans, its newsletter, speeches made by the administrator, the institute's program of technology transfer, its "exemplary project" designation, and many informal procedures that provide incentives and communicate values.

[2]Robert Cushman, "LEAA's 'Pilot Cities'—A Model for Criminal Justice Research and Demonstration," *San Diego Law Review*, 9, June 1972, p. 753.

[3]Ibid., p. 756.

[4]Ibid., p. 755.

[5]U. S. General Accounting Office, *The Pilot Cities Program: Phaseout Needed Due to Limited National Benefits*, B-171019 (Washington, D. C.: Government Printing Office, Feb. 3, 1975), p. 32.

[6]Ibid.

[7]Ibid., p. 23.

[8]Ibid., p. 27. See also, pp. 25, 30.

[9]Ibid., p. 20.

[10]*Fourth Annual Report of LEAA* (Washington, D. C.: Government Printing Office, 1972), p. 3.

[11]*LEAA Newsletter*, vol. 2, no. 4, March 1972, p. 4.

[12]*LEAA Newsletter*, vol. 2, no. 8, Aug. 1972, p. 1.

[13]The MITRE Corporation Criminal Justice Evaluation (project leader, Eleanor Chelimsky), *The High Impact Anti-Crime Program: National-Level Evaluation, An Interim Summary Report of Program Status and Evaluation Findings to Date* (draft), July 1, 1975, pp. 7–8.

[14]Ibid., pp. 6–7.

[15]Ibid., p. 14.

[16]Ibid.

[17]Ibid., p. 22.

[18]Ibid., p. 18.

[19]R. Cole, "Revenue Sharing: Citizen Participation in Social Service Aspects," *The Annals*, May 1975, p. 69.

[20]*Sixth Annual Report of LEAA* (Washington, D. C.: Government Printing Office, 1974), p. 97.

[21]Ibid.

[22]E. E. Schattschneider, *The Semisovereign People* (New York: Holt, Reinhart and Winston, 1961).

[23]James Q. Wilson, *Thinking about Crime* (New York: Basic Books, 1975), p. 208.

[24]*LEAA Newsletter*, vol. 5, no. 2, Aug. 1975, p. 8.

Chapter IV

[1]U. S. General Accounting Office, *Problems in Administering Programs to Improve Law Enforcement Education*, GGD-75-67 (Washington, D. C.: Government Printing Office, June 11, 1975), p. 25.

[2]Ibid., pp. 25–26.

[3]Title I, Sec. 402 (b).

[4]*LEAA Newsletter*, vol. 2, no. 1, Nov. 1971, p. 1.

[5]Ibid., p. 3.

[6]Twelve task forces functioned under the National Advisory Commission. They dealt, respectively, with Police; Courts; Corrections; Community Crime Prevention; Civil Disorders; Community Involvement; Drug Abuse; Education, Training, and Manpower Development; Information Systems and Statistics; Juvenile Delinquency; Organized Crime; and Research and Development. The commission has published its findings in seven volumes: *The Criminal Justice System; Police; Courts; Corrections; A National Strategy to Reduce Crime; Community Crime Prevention*; and *The Proceedings of the National Conference on Criminal Justice* (Washington, D. C.: Government Printing Office, Jan. 23, 1973).

[7]*LEAA Newsletter*, vol. 3, no. 7, Sept.–Oct. 1973, p. 3.

[8]National Advisory Commission on Criminal Justice Standards and Goals, *Police*, p. 97.

[9]Ibid., p. 206.

[10]*LEAA Newsletter*, vol. 3, no. 10, Jan.–Feb. 1974, p. 12.

[11]*Computerworld*, Feb. 3, 1971.

[12]Project SEARCH, *International Symposium on Criminal Justice Information and Statistics Systems* (Washington, D. C.: Government Printing Office, Oct. 1972), p. 18.

[13]*Sixth Annual Report of LEAA* (Washington, D. C.: Government Printing Office, 1974), p. 75.

[14]Hannah Shields and Mae Churchill, "The Fraudulent War on Crime," *The Nation*, Dec. 21, 1974, p. 650.

[15]*Sixth Annual Report of LEAA*, p. 82.

[16]*The New York Times*, Oct. 29, 1975, p. 20.

[17]Letter from John Tunney to Harold Tyler, July 18, 1975.

[18]Letter from Harold Tyler to John Tunney, Aug. 29, 1975.

[19]Shields and Churchill, op. cit., p. 651.

[20]*Standards for Security and Privacy of Criminal Justice Information*, Technical Report No. 13 (Sacramento, Calif.: SEARCH Group, Inc., October 1975), p. 1 (subsequently referred to as *Standards*).

[21]*Standards*, p. 27.

[22]The following are some important recommendations in *Standards:*

- Federal legislation should be made applicable to all but purely intrastate systems.

- Traditionally public criminal justice information—police blotters, court records of public proceedings, traffic offenses, and statistics in which individuals are not identified—should not be subject to the recommended legislation.

- Criminal justice agencies should be allowed to continue to make to the press factual statements about investigations in progress.

- Information systems containing more than 10,000 records should be required to publish annual notices apprising the public of their existence and general content.

- Correctional and release information should be made available *only* to criminal justice agencies and subjects of such information.

- Intelligence and investigative information should be segregated from criminal justice information.

- Direct access to information systems should be strictly limited to authorized offices within criminal justice agencies.

- Arrest records should be made available only for limited purposes such as employment by law enforcement agencies or determinations for pretrial release and for routine purposes *only* in cases in which the outcome is a conviction or a guilty plea.

- Limitations should be imposed on the availability of criminal justice information for non-criminal justice governmental employment.

- Criminal justice records should not be released to employers, credit bureaus, etc., except at the request of the individual subject or in a narrow range of situations controlled by state statute or court order.

- Individuals should have complete access to their files and to transcripts of administrative hearings and judicial reviews for the purpose of challenging information contained in them.

- No individual should be required to pass on his file to any other person. (Employers in some areas have skirted privacy requirements by making applicants request and turn over their files as a condition of employment.)

- The maintenance and dissemination of intelligence and investigative information should be rigidly controlled and periodically reviewed, and such information should be destroyed after a fixed interval if no criminal prosecution is brought.

- Criminal justice personnel should be allowed to relate the substance of the subject's correctional and release file at the request of the subject.

- Direct access to information by remote terminal should be limited to requests identifying specific individuals or categories of offenses and to those criminal justice agencies whose procedures ensure that such information is used only in relation to a particular criminal investigation.

- The physical security of the system should be ensured.

- All records should be updated to reflect disposition after arrest. When information is updated or modified, the identity of the supplier of information should be confirmed, and logs as to the suppliers and users of the information should be kept for three years.

- Records should be sealed or purged after a specific time (seven years after a felony with no further arrests, five years after a misdemeanor with no further arrests).

- A National Interstate Information system should be established, housing only records on subjects of legitimate federal concern (for example, violators of federal law and criminals with records in more than one state).

- A national justice information board should be established to implement and enforce privacy and security legislation.

- Where state law is more restrictive and protective of privacy interests, it should govern, but in all other interstate situations, federal legislation should govern.

- Civil, administrative, and criminal penalties should be established for violations of the safeguards.

[23]*Standards*, pp. 2 (ff.), 7.
[24]Ibid., p. 26.
[25]See Title I, Sec. 524 (b).

Chapter V

[1]See Graham W. Watt, "The Goals and Objectives of General Revenue Sharing," *The Annals*, vol. 419, May 1975, pp. 12–13. See also, 31 U.S.C. (Supp. II) §1224 (b).
[2]Richard P. Nathan, Dan Crippen, and Andre Juneau, "Where Have All the Dollars Gone—Implications of Revenue Sharing for the Law Enforcement Assistance Act," Department of Justice, LEAA (draft), Oct. 31, 1975, p. 10.
[3]Title I, Sec. 303 (c).
[4]Transcript of press conference held by Governor Edmund G. Brown, Jr., April 2, 1975.
[5]Letter from LEAA regional office in San Francisco to Gray Davis (Governor Brown's assistant), May 15, 1975.
[6]Testimony of Slade Gortin, attorney general of the state of Washington, U. S., Congress, Senate, Judiciary Committee, Subcommittee on Criminal Laws and Procedures, Oct. 8, 1975.
[7]Testimony of Mayor Harvey Sloan, M.D., on behalf of the National League of Cities–U. S. Conference of Mayors, U. S., Congress, Senate, Judiciary Committee, Subcommittee on Criminal Laws and Procedures, Oct. 9, 1975.
[8]Testimony of Wes Wise, on behalf of the National League of Cities–U. S. Conference of Mayors, U. S., Congress, Senate, Judiciary Committee, Subcommittee on Criminal Laws and Procedures, Oct. 9, 1975.
[9]Testimony of Wayne F. Anderson, David B. Walker, and Carl W. Stenberg,

on behalf of the Advisory Commission on Intergovernmental Relations, U. S., Congress, Senate, Judiciary Committee, Subcommittee on Criminal Laws and Procedures, Oct. 22, 1975.

[10]Minutes of the board meeting of the New York Crime Control Planning Board, As to No. 2051—Troy—Citizen Participation–Crime Control, New York City, Sept. 5, 1975.

[11]Testimony of MacFarlane.

[12]Committee on Government Operations, Twelfth Report, *Block Grant Programs in the Law Enforcement Assistance Administration*, 92nd Cong., 2nd Sess., May 18, 1972, H. Rept. 92–1072, p. 8. See also, pp. 70–77.

[13]Charles Work, speech before the National State Criminal Justice Planning Administrators Conference meeting, Denver, Colo., Nov. 19, 1975.

[14]Ilene N. Bernstein and John Cardascia, "Strategies and Design for Criminal Justice Evaluation," draft of Paper delivered at American Sociology Association meeting, San Francisco, Calif., Oct. 1975.

[15]Robert Martinson, "What Works?—Questions and Answers about Prison Reform," *The Public Interest*, no. 35, Spring 1974, p. 23.

[16]"Residential Community Corrections Programs: A Preliminary Evaluation," prepared by the Evaluation Unit of the Governor's Commission on Crime Prevention and Control, Minnesota, April 1975.

[17]Ibid.

[18]Ibid.

[19]"Response to Preliminary Report of Evaluation Unit on Residential Community Corrections Programs," prepared by the Minnesota Department of Corrections, May 15, 1975.

[20]Richard A. Berk and Peter H. Rossi, "Doing Good or Worse: Evaluation Research Politically Reexamined," Paper delivered at Joint Session of American Sociology Association and Society for the Study of Social Problems, San Francisco, Calif., Aug. 1975.

[21]Criminal Courts Technical Assistance Project of American University, *Report of the Special Study Team on LEAA Support of the State Courts* (Washington, D. C.: Department of Justice, LEAA, Oct. 1975), Contract no. J-LEAA-043-72, pp. 42–65.

[22]Title I, Sec. 303 (a) (11).

Chapter VI

[1]James Q. Wilson, op. cit.

[2]Testimony of Harris.

[3]Testimony of Amos A. Reed, on behalf of the Association of State Correctional Administrators, U. S., Congress, Senate, Judiciary Committee, Subcommittee on Criminal Laws and Procedures, Nov. 4, 1975.

[4]Edward M. Kennedy, Opening Remarks on the LEAA Reauthorization Hearings, U. S., Congress, Senate, Judiciary Committee, Subcommittee on Criminal Laws and Procedures, Oct. 3, 1975.

[5]National Conference of State Criminal Justice Planning Administrators, op. cit., p. 3.

[6]Testimony of Anderson, Walker, and Stenberg.

[7]Background Paper prepared for the Conference on Crime Control and Criminal Justice Research at Harvard Law School, Cambridge, Mass., May 15–16, 1975.

[8]Joseph L. White, *NCCD Criminal Justice Newsletter*, July 7, 1975.

[9]American Civil Liberties Union complaint in *National Black Police Association v. Velde*, 75 Civ. 1444 (D.D.C., filed Sept. 4, 1975), p. 51.

[10]Testimony of Aryeh Neier, on behalf of the American Civil Liberties Union, U. S., Congress, Senate, Judiciary Committee, Subcommittee on Criminal Laws and Procedures, Oct. 23, 1975.

[11]U. S., Congress, House, 119, *Congressional Record*, 20071, 1973.

[12]Title I, Sec. 518 (c).

[13]Ibid.

[14]Ibid.

[15]Letter from Richard Larson, staff attorney with the American Civil Liberties Union, to the authors, Oct. 30, 1975.

[16]Martha Derthick, *The Influence of Federal Grants* (Cambridge, Mass.: Harvard University Press, 1970), p. 207.

[17]28 C.F.R. Sec. 42.201 et seq., Subpart D, published in the *Federal Register*, Aug. 18, 1972.

[18]Jacques K. Boyer and Edward Griggs, *Equal Employment Opportunity Program Development Manual* (Washington, D. C.: Department of Justice, LEAA Office of Civil Rights Compliance, July 1974).

[19]Larson, op. cit.

[20]*Sixth Annual Report of LEAA*, p. 73.

[21]Proposed regulations published in the *Federal Register*, vol. 40, no. 98, May 20, 1975, p. 22114.

[22]Letter from Gordon Zenk to authors, Nov. 7, 1975.

[23]Testimony of Neier.

[24]Ronald Sullivan, "Rodino Pressure on U. S. Reported," *The New York Times*, Feb. 17, 1976, p. 1.